D1327240

Shakespeare *Without Words*

AND OTHER ESSAYS

Shakespeare Without Words
AND OTHER ESSAYS

ALFRED HARBAGE

HARVARD UNIVERSITY PRESS

CAMBRIDGE, MASSACHUSETTS . 1972

© COPYRIGHT 1972 BY THE
PRESIDENT AND FELLOWS OF HARVARD COLLEGE
ALL RIGHTS RESERVED

Publication of this book has been aided by a grant from the Hyder Edward Rollins Fund

LIBRARY OF CONGRESS CATALOG CARD NUMBER 77-188353

SBN 674-80395-7

PRINTED IN THE UNITED STATES OF AMERICA

LIBRARY
FLORIDA STATE UNIVERSITY
TALLAHASSEE, FLORIDA

To my former colleagues and to alumni
of the drama seminars

FOREWORD

*A*T THE courteous prompting of some of the dedicatees I have assembled these essays on Shakespeare and his fellows. They are presented in two groups: those which I hope still have critical interest, and those which I hope still have historical utility. My original plan was to exclude articles pre senting unarguable and hence uninteresting facts, introduc- tions to editions and anthologies prepared by myself or others, and contributions to volumes honoring scholars in the field. However, when I found that my sponsors wanted them in, I decided that including a few *Festschrift* offerings would not be Indian-giving but a way of honoring the receivers twice.

"Shakespeare Without Words" and "Marlowe Disinterred" were instigated by books which are already sinking toward the horizon, but my strictures are aimed less at these par- ticular books than at what they represent. It is still high noon for pseudo-Shakespeareana as a class. Of more dubious rele- vance is "Cosmic Card Game." It is a parody. The fact may seem too obvious for remark, but some of its original readers failed to recognize it as such and sent letters of protest to the editor of *The American Scholar.* (One correspondent was especially incensed by the disparaging allusion to Professor Kittredge.) I no longer feel ill-disposed toward the New Critics, the best of whom were trying to express old truths in a novel way. The last paragraph of my exercise, which I once thought the cream of my jest upon the New Criticism, now strikes me as almost a tribute to it.

The essays of the second group are exploratory, intended to suggest areas which may repay further research. Shakespeare's theatrical milieu is and must remain a realm of the imper· fectly known, revealed to us only in broken glimpses. We have most of the best of the plays, but must piece out as best we can our knowledge of the authors and audiences responsible for their creation. If I here seem to be doing the kind of thing I have elsewhere rebuked others for doing, I can only say, in emulation of Burke, that when foolish men guess the wise must conjecture. I have shrunk from the considerable task of rechecking the data in the final article, but the original manuscript was read by Ronald McKerrow, who is unlikely to have missed major inaccuracies of fact.

The British Academy lecture, which gives its title to the collection, has been revised in an attempt to improve its style. "Shakespeare Interred?" "Extricating the Sonnets," and "Sparrow from Stratford" are new titles, and almost new essays, since only a few paragraphs of the originals have been retained intact. Only minor revisions appear in the remaining pieces. I wish to thank the original publishers, indicated in the notes, for permission to reprint.

Cherry Hill, New Jersey   A. H.

CONTENTS

I

II

PART I

1 SHAKESPEARE WITHOUT WORDS

*S*HAKESPEARE's plays would not have been enjoyed if they had offended the moral and religious sentiments prevailing in the audience for which they were designed. A basic conformity with the current system of values must be assumed. The system was submitted to tests, perilously near the breaking point in a tragedy such as *Lear,* but this testing was a feature of the artistry, not a covert form of didacticism. To say that the system does not *really* meet the tests is to say that these are not *really* Renaissance plays but are, in fact, twentieth-century satires. It is useless to speculate upon the extent to which Shakespeare deferred to the system other than as an artist, or upon its influence on his personal conduct. Our best clue to his attitude toward it is the success with which he manipulated it. He must have accorded the system the respect and affection which artists usually accord their materials. He must have felt "at home" with it.

It may be argued that an equivalent attitude is the condition of a spontaneous response; that is, we must feel "at home" with the system of values informing the plays and be distracted by no impulse either to attack or defend it. When we speak of Shakespeare's "universality" we imply that this is possible—that the moral and religious sentiments assimilated in his art are recognizable and congenial in all times and places. But when we examine the testimony of different times and places, as expressed in Shakespearean commentary, we must wonder what is meant by his "universality," if it means anything at all.

The Annual Shakespeare Lecture of The British Academy, delivered in London, April 23, 1969, and printed in *Proceedings of The British Academy,* vol. 55 (London, Oxford University Press, 1970).

I do not refer to the historical allowances that must be made. Foreigners are not necessarily repelled by Shakespeare's political insularity, his British nationalism. Certain values are expressed in an idiom of limited currency, and we may properly say that the *universal* value implicit in Shakespeare's nationalism is affection for and a sense of obligation to the society of which one is a member. The socially alienated are more likely than the nationally alien to be put off by this particular Shakespearean value. But the penetration to underlying values must observe a stopping point. If we find an ultimate acquiescence in anarchy expressed in the history plays, we have not penetrated but have punctured them. Such is true also if we find in the comedies and tragedies a covert leaning toward the kind of sexual permissiveness endorsed by many twentieth-century writers. Actually a strict code is subsumed, with chastity accepted as a virtue. We may say that here the underlying value is constancy, as it mainly is, but in sexual conduct constancy and promiscuity are incompatible, as in wider areas of human relationship civility and nationalism are not. Of course constancy may be rejected as a virtue, at least in the privileged area of sexual expression, but the rejection carries with it the obligation to concede a large element of obsolescence in Shakespeare's comedies and tragedies. (I assume candor to be a virtue.)

In the history of a work of literary art one or both of two things may happen: we may reject the system of values conditioning its original creation, or we may cease to understand the idiom in which the system is expressed. By effort we can learn the idiom. But by no amount of effort can we recover sympathy with the discarded system of values to the extent that we can enjoy its presence. Spontaneous enjoyment of the work must decrease in proportion to this loss of sympathy, and when the loss is complete the work is no longer alive. It may have a posthumous existence in the museum-theatre and the library, affording the attenuated pleasure taken in technique abstracted from content, but wholeness has departed from the work as when a soul has left a body. It cannot be revived by new "interpretation," however weirdly it may be made to gyrate in the hands of the body-snatchers.

Strangely enough, the receding acceptability of a system of values is signaled by those who rise to defend it as well as those who try to convert it into something more to their taste. As a case in point we may take the Shakespearean code of sexual conduct mentioned above. Critics have protested too much, or have averted their eyes, or have substituted their own predilections. An uncertainty of response became apparent when the later Victorian critics began to lecture upon chastity as from a Shakespearean platform; their praises of Imogen's purity would have made Imogen blush, and wonder how, as the loving wife and the redeemer of the play, they had expected her to behave. Later came the tendency to avoid the subject. One may read in recent books praises of Prospero in many imposing roles, from art impresario to hierophant, but never as the stern preacher to Ferdinand and Miranda on the text of premarital continence. His views in this area have evidently become embarrassing. And (last scene of all) Shakespeare has now been listed in a magazine for the cultivated as one of the world's "great pornographers."[1] The writer was no doubt aware of the ribald puns in the plays and sonnets, and of the titles of the narrative poems: he needed nothing more than goodwill.

Shakespearean criticism has always been, in the main, a record of the nature of the response to the moral stimulus provided by the plays, and is chiefly interesting as an index of cultural history. My concern here is with the present moment in cultural history, and what a certain kind of Shake-

[1] Brendan Gill, "The Unfinished Man," *New Yorker*, March 8, 1969, p. 119.

5

spearean criticism seems to be telling us about it. The kind I have in mind is more doctrinal than the criticism of the moralizing Victorians, and far more egocentric. Sometimes we are told what the plays would mean if the critic or his favorite ideologue had written them. And sometimes we seem to be watching a game of critical scrabble, with the contestants each taking a handful of pieces from the plays and combining them in novel ways. The deviser of the greatest number of unlikely combinations is declared the winner of the game.

The uniqueness, indeed the *identity* of a work of art resides in its composition—that is, in relationships rather than in the parts related, whether lines, masses, colors, sounds, words, mimetic actions, whatever it may be. To convert a Shakespearean play into doctrine entails the ignoring of relationships while attention is focused upon selected parts. At the most elementary level of analysis a play consists of action and accompanying words. To ignore the action is impossible, because without it, seen on the stage or visualized in the study, there is no play but only a sequence of miscellaneous utterances. To ignore the words is possible, once the action has been become available through reading, playgoing, or common report. We must agree, however, that to interpret the action in disregard of the words is an extreme form of selectivity, available only to the most ruthless type of exegete. That such a type has emerged, and that his presence among us is embarrassing if not ominous, I shall presently maintain, but let me illustrate first the mere intelligibility of Shakespeare without words.

I shall give two illustrations: the first, the simplest I can think of, the Epilogue to *The Tempest;* and the second, one of the most complex, Gloucester's attempted suicide in *King Lear.* The first is simple because it is not an integral part of the play, but a conventional appendage to it. Viewed simply as an action it does not affect any preceding action, and, of course, no action follows it by which it might be affected. First let us hear the words which we will presently ignore. Prospero has given up his magical powers after using them to right ancient wrongs. His enemies have fallen into his hands, have been punished enough to induce penitence, at least in some, and have then been forgiven. His daughter is provided with a suitable husband, and he is ready to return to his recovered dukedom:

> Now my Charmes are all ore-throwne,
> And what strength I haue's mine owne.
> Which is most faint: now 'tis true
> I must be heere confinde by you,
> Or sent to Naples, Let me not
> Since I haue my Dukedome got,
> And pardon'd the deceiuer, dwell
> In this bare Island, by your Spell,
> But release me from my bands
> With the helpe of your good hands:
> Gentle breath of yours, my Sailes
> Must fill, or else my proiect failes,
> Which was to please: Now I want
> Spirits to enforce: Art to inchant,
> And my ending is despaire,
> Vnlesse I be relieu'd by praier
> Which peirces so, that it assaults
> Mercy it selfe, and frees all faults.
> > As you from crimes would pardon'd be,
> > Let your Indulgence set me free.

The indicated action comes as near as any in Shakespeare to being fully intelligible without words. The one who has played Prospero moves to the forefront of the stage, faces the audience, and makes a gesture of humility. The action is only a bow. The genesis of the gesture of humility after a display of power, in theatre, circus, concert hall, bullring, is a mystery I need not try to explain. Perhaps in its origins the bow was an act of propitiation to the people as delegates of the envious gods, but we need think of it now only as a thing of custom—a response to or a plea for approval. A performer's bow is a brave and hopeful thing, the reverse of a gesture of despair.

What, then, is a critic to make of it when he is extracting from *The Tempest* signals of despair? This bow will not serve his turn. Needing more than the action, he turns to the words, but finds them the exact equivalent of the action, an ingratiating testament of hope. His resort is to proceed without some of them, and he quotes the Epilogue thus:

> Now I want
> Spirits to enforce: Art to inchant,
> And my ending is despaire ...

I would be ashamed to offer this in illustration were not the Epilogue exactly so used not once but three times, at the beginning, middle, and end of a chapter in the most fashionable book of Shakespearean commentary of the past decade.[2] Now to change the meaning of a sentence by stopping it in midcareer is, as Prince Hamlet would say, as easy as lying, and a proper occasion for rebuke—but who is in a sound position to administer it? There is truly a vein of melancholy perceptible in *The Tempest,* and it may be that the former insistence that the play represents Shakespeare "on the heights" itself smacked of the doctrinal. Strachey was reacting to this earlier simplification when he insisted that it revealed not a resurgent but a "bored" Shakespeare. Commonplaces invite that lowest form of originality, commonplaces reversed.

[2] Jan Kott, *Shakespeare Our Contemporary,* trans. Boleslaw Taborski (New York, 1964), pp. 166, 193, 205.

In truth the words of this Epilogue defy doctrinal deployment. If they provide no text for the pessimist, neither do they for the optimist, whether Marxian or Christian. Imagine a committee of comrades gazing gloomily at the remainder of the broken sentence—

> Vnlesse I be relieu'd by praier
> Which pierces so, that it assaults
> Mercy it selfe, and frees all faults.

Who can be rebuked for erasing this metaphysical babble, in which "despaire" is coupled with "mercy" in an orthodox Christian paradigm? The Christian exegete will be equally baffled. As a symbolic action this bow is insufficiently specific, and as a structure of words it is specific in the wrong direction. The words form an ingenious conceit, saying that the breeze generated by applauding hands will fill the sails that are to waft Prospero to Naples. True, the Lord's Prayer is paraphrased, but not to pious ends. An Elizabethan divine of any sect would have been incensed: this is not Christian doctrine but players' blackmail, equating failure to applaud this silly play with failure to endorse the Lord's Prayer. Earnest men since have stoutly denied that Shakespeare himself could have written this frivolous Epilogue: it is an addition by an inferior hand. Those more relaxed in their responses have enjoyed it as a graceful bow, and one suggesting that Shakespeare, or his audience, or both were reasonably well disposed toward the Christian faith.

As an action becomes more complex, in itself and in relation to other actions in a play, the consequence of ignoring some or all of the accompanying words becomes increasingly spectacular. In *King Lear* we see a ragged young man lead a blinded old one to a spot on a level stage. By the young man's gestures we know that he has deceived the old man into thinking that they stand on the edge of a precipice. The old man gives him a purse, then leaps into the imaginary void, only to fall on his face. Then the young man arouses him, and we know by further gestures that he succeeds in another deception, making the old man believe that he lies at the foot of the precipice, yet miraculously remains alive. What can be made of this action? A small child will see in it something comical. Raggedness is comical, blindness more comical, and falling on one's face most comical of all. That a residue of this relish for distress in others survives to later years no one can deny, and if we are victims of arrested moral development so that we have come to love cruelty for its own sake, we will find the action fully intelligible as a display of ingenious cruelty. The young man has teased an aged sufferer, and kept him alive so that he may suffer more. Or what if we are *practical-minded*? We have observed that the young man has received a purse. Obviously he is keeping the old one alive in the hope of extracting more swag.

Further vistas open when this action is viewed in relation to earlier ones. We know that the young man has been misused by the old man, and we conclude that his cruel teasing is his way of getting revenge. Or suppose that we have heard so much of Shakespeare's powers of characterization that we can think of nothing else. In an earlier action the old man was duped by his younger son. In the present action he is duped by his elder son. The same old gullible Gloucester! How *clever* Shakespeare is! If we add to the action of this play actions we recall from others, the range of interpretation becomes staggering. We watch Shakespeare's pair of outcasts, the ragged leading the blind, from whom even the comfort of death is ludicrously snatched away; and we were once deeply impressed by a piece from the hand of a modern Irish playwright in which two tramps are displayed as the clownish victims of a cruel cosmic joke exploiting their delusions about a better world to come. I refer, of course, to Lord Dunsany's

The Glittering Gate—not a profound work, as its author would have been the first to admit, yet one carrying most of the philosophical stock-in-trade of our present theatre of the absurd.[3] Seeing the action of Gloucester's attempted suicide in terms of the action of *The Glittering Gate* lets us reach a simple conclusion: *King Lear* advances the doctrine of mankind's destiny as clownish victim of cosmic cruelty.

My point is that the action of a Shakespearean play has more meaning, or at least more meanings, without the words than with them. The words are a limiting factor, obtruding upon our view what it may still be permissible to refer to as the author's intention. In the present case, when we restore the words uttered during Gloucester's attempted suicide, we find the equivalent of restoring the word "Mercy" after "despaire" in the Epilogue to *The Tempest;* this is, we must again reckon with Christian eschatology. The moment of Gloucester's resolution to take his own life is signaled by his words,

> As Flies to wanton Boyes, are we to th' Gods,
> They kill vs for their sport. (IV. i. 36–37)

The lines are often cited, their dramatic function rarely. They mark Gloucester's surrender to despair, the unpardonable sin. The motive for Edgar's behavior as the two stand above the imaginary void is stated explicitly:

> Why I do trifle thus with his dispaire,
> Is done to cure it. (IV. vi. 33–34)

In a religious sense the void is not imaginary. The cure is successful. Told that the one who has consented to lead him to its brink bore the aspect of a fiend, Gloucester abjures suicide:

[3] Observe the elaboration of the theme in the various plays of Dunsany's compatriot, Samuel Beckett.

> ... henceforth Ile beare
> Affliction, till it do cry out it selfe
> Enough, enough, and dye. (IV. vi. 75–76)

The action ends with Edgar's pious counsel: "Beare free [i.e. innocent] and patient thoughts" (IV. vi. 80).

The presence of Edgar in *King Lear* embarrasses expounders of the play's nihilism. What is a person like him doing in a place like this? Cordelia is less inconvenient, since she perishes, but Edgar survives, succeeds, and stands as a power symbol at the conclusion of the play. Observe, however, that he also proves none too tractable as a displaced Christian. He returns good for evil, and saves his father's soul, but at the expense of a prodigious lot of deceit, including the faking of a miracle. Or is this in fact the total impression conveyed? Is a miracle which succeeds a fake? What is a miracle anyway? Thomas More once told of a miracle he had seen with his own eyes.[4] An apprentice and a tradesman's daughter plighted their troth, married, and set up housekeeping in Cheapside, whereupon an amazing thing happened. In nine months' time these two people became three. More's straight-faced proof that millions of miracles are happening every day lends a kind of sanction. If a future saint may grow playful with miracles, why not a popular playwright?

I have not tried to demonstrate that *King Lear* preaches Christianity or even Christian humanism. Those to whom the complex of values referred to as Christian humanism remains recognizable and even dear are apt to explicate Shakespeare in its terms. When accused of converting the play into dogma and Shakespeare into a theologian, their feelings are understandably hurt, especially when the charge comes from persons who share their ethical and religious loyalties. In this

---

[4] Thomas More, *A Dialogue concernynge heresyes & matters of religion,* 1528, chap. 10.

dispute one may sympathize with both the accusers and the accused, with the latter because they are responding to a stimulus truly present in the plays, and with the former because they are trying to keep Shakespeare clear of the doctrinal wars. They know that, if tested as a theologian, Shakespeare will not pass, and there will be laughter under the hills. Their cautionary role is itself open to misunderstanding. The idea that anyone or anything may be nondoctrinally, unmilitantly humanistic and Christian seems very hard to grasp. It is as hard to define as the nature of art itself. Upon one thing I should insist: that those who are aware of Christian humanism as a frame of reference in Shakespeare's plays are unable to misconstrue them with the thoroughness of those who are not.

We are sometimes told that the way a work of art appeared in its own age, even to its maker, is irrelevant. A great work is autonomous and has the chameleon's faculty of altering with its environment: it is what it appears to be to the perceptive modern observer. The principle is seductive because it flatters everyone—the modern observer because he figures as re-creator, and the original artist because he wrought better than he knew. It is also convenient because it lets one palm off one's own creations as masterpieces of the past. I am reminded of Turgenev's Bazarov. Ironically presented as a man with the courage to believe in nothing, he believes firmly in his own ideas. He begins by dismissing the works of Pushkin as twaddle, but later proceeds to attribute to Pushkin his own aphorisms. Bazarov believes in the usefulness of prestige.

The principle of the autonomy of art reduces itself in practice to the truism that all objects may be converted from their original uses. A trash incinerator may be used to burn all the books in the British Museum, but we would speak of its "autonomy" only if we wished to see them burned. A guillotine could be used to slice ham if we were willing to put up with its inconvenient dimensions. The statement that a work of art is seen differently in different ages is a statistical generalization having nothing to do with the justice with which individuals see it. Even in its own age it is seen differently by different people, with some seeing it more justly than others. The only valid test for determining how justly a work of art is seen, in its own age or later, is the measurement of how much of its data is taken into account. In the case of a Shakespearean play, the data consist of the words, the actions, and their relationships. Those who speak of the autonomy inherent in its complexity invariably proceed to simplify it by a process of reduction. The ultimate reduction involves dismissal of the words. With the action freely interpretable, any Shakespearean play can be relocated in the modern theatre of the absurd.

The notion of Shakespeare as writer for a theatre of the absurd is not new. Voltaire saw him more or less in this light. In 1837 Chateaubriand called *Hamlet* the "tragedy of maniacs"—". . . that Royal Bedlam in which every character is either crazy or criminal, . . . and in which the grave itself furnishes the stage with the skull of a fool; that Odeon of shadows and specters, where we hear nothing but reveries, the challenge of sentinels, the screeching of the nightbird, and the roaring of the sea."[5] The work thus piquantly described was, of course, available in the theatre, provided one was able to pay the admission fee and was unable to understand English. What is being described is a *Hamlet* without words, a pantomimic *Hamlet* of sights and sound effects. Except for the latter and certain "reveries" (presumably the detachable soliloquies) we "hear nothing."

Although not quite freed from the influence of Voltaire, Chateaubriand was being playful. In what I mentioned above

[5] François René de Chateaubriand, *Sketches of English Literature* (London, 1837), p. 276.

as the most fashionable book of Shakespearean commentary of the past decade, the reduction of the plays to pantomime with "reveries" (in this case the critic's own) is not playful. What emerges is a series of history plays in which automaton kings are cranked into lethal action by a senselessly cruel machine. *Macbeth* is one of those "history" plays, with no distinction perceptible between the occasion of the Thane's killing others and the occasion of his being killed. *King Lear* is a grotesque charade, presenting no tragic hero but only a clutch of writhing clowns. *A Midsummer Night's Dream* is an exploration of lechery, in particular bestiality. *The Tempest* is a sigh of despair. You will have identified the book as Jan Kott's *Shakespeare Our Contemporary*. Its method is to ignore Shakespeare's words except for those taken out of context, as in the quotation from Prospero's Epilogue. Elsewhere an action will be described, classified as a "mime," and then interpreted in terms of a work by some artist other than Shakespeare. While Titania and Bottom dream, we get a graphic account of the sexual depravities depicted in Goya's *Caprichos*. By this means Shakespeare becomes "our contemporary." A few details are justly described, but these have long since figured prominently in Shakespearean commentary. All that is valid in the chapter on *King Lear* was expressed in one striking image and a brief following paragraph by Edward Dowden in 1875.

When I read *Shakespeare Our Contemporary* and watched Amurath to Amurath succeeding, and Krafft-Ebing's *Psychopathia Sexualis* dramatized in the woods outside Athens, and Prospero dragging his dejected form through the landscape of Hieronymus Bosch, my response was precisely what might be expected from the elderly innocent I am—angry indignation. But this emotion was soon recollected in relative tranquility, since it was succeeded by curiosity. What would the response to this view of Shakespeare reveal about the temper of our times? A full history of this response would, as I soon discovered, require the labors of a multilingual committee working full time for many months; but I am able to supply an outline. Those who discussed the book in print divided into three groups. First, and quite small in number, were those who dismissed it as worthless. Their number would perhaps be augmented if we could add those who refused to review it, wistfully trusting that their silence would be construed as stony. Of this remnant I shall say no more, but leave them with my respectful salute.

In a second and larger group, made up mainly of academics, judgment was hedged with qualifications. The professional Shakespeareans are aware that Shakespeare's scenarios (as distinct from his texts) are often sensational, farcical, fanciful, or a combination of the three which may properly be called grotesque. They are also aware, at least some of them, that in certain Elizabethan plays one finds complete or almost complete congruence of scenario and text. In the case of *The Revenger's Tragedy* as distinct from *Hamlet,* and in the case of most of the plays of Marston, performance in pantomime would convey virtually the same impression as performance with words. The language is distinguished, but in a sense redundant, since it fails to modify the impression of the grotesque conveyed by the sensational, farcical, and fanciful action. The Elizabethans truly had their theatre of the absurd, a small one, but its plays lack the prestige to be viable in its modern counterpart. No one seems to care whether Marston is "our contemporary." Now the scholarly reviewers, conscious of those features which Shakespeare's plays share with the lesser kind of their day, felt impelled to follow a judicious line; the key phrase in their appraisals was that Kott had gone "too far." I must confess that judiciousness of this kind strikes me as a conditioned reflex rather than a working principle; if someone is headed in the wrong direction, is not his first step "too far"? However, I am an academic man myself and can understand the leaning toward yes-and-no judgments. There is always the fear that blunt disapproval, a downright no, will smack of dogmatism or seem to abrogate the right of free speech; perhaps this is a new infirmity of noble minds.

The third and by far most numerous group of responders greeted the book with enthusiastic approval. For the most part they were theatrical and literary journalists, those who preside over one branch of the arts by directing plays, conducting book columns, and writing reviews for periodicals. In their occupation an espousal of the contemporary is a condition of employment, and one can sympathize with their elation at the discovery of so reputable a contemporary as Shakespeare; why look this gift horse in the mouth? A significant feature of their response was their common assumption that some playwrights are more contemporary than others, with Genet, Ionesco, Beckett, and so forth, the most contemporary of all. Also significant was the fact that the welcome given by the intelligentsia to the idea of a dark, destructive Shakespeare stopped short at the border of the Soviet Union. Although Kott's book met with a mixed or favorable response everywhere from Sweden to Israel and from Czechoslovakia to Japan, it was viewed as ratsbane by the Russians. A rival book by a Russian critic, Grigori Kozintsev, reinvoked the more familiar Shakespeare, bright apostle of moral decency and the dignity of man.[6] It is called in English translation *Shakespeare: Time and Conscience,* but was published in Russian as *Our Contemporary: William Shakespeare.* One is bound to ask whether the kind of "contemporary" that Shakespeare proves to be depends less on when one lives than on where one lives. Or putting it another

[6] Grigori Kozintsev, *Shakespeare: Time and Conscience,* trans. Joyce Vining (New York, 1966).

way: is there now a "Shakespeare West" and a "Shakespeare East"?

Here I must say a word about recent Shakespearean criticism in the Soviet Union. Until 1940 this criticism was dogmatically Marxist, with Shakespeare accepted as a literary genius, but one who spoke for a dying aristocracy—or else a rising bourgeoisie. The emphasis then shifted, and Shakespeare was viewed as spokesman for the common humanity which had been victimized by feudalism and was about to be victimized by capitalism. The emphasis has now shifted so far that the Marxist element is scarcely visible. Shakespeare preached nothing, but his frame of reference was (this may come as a surprise) Christian humanism. The Russians do not call it Christian humanism; they call it *popular* humanism, but it amounts to the same thing in their appraisal of the ethical thrust of Shakespearean drama. They prefer to cite folktales, ballads, fables, and proverbs in illustrating Shakespeare's humanism, instead of the texts of the clerical reformers favored by Western Renaissance scholars, but they are aware of those texts and no longer refrain from occasionally mentioning God. This body of current Russian criticism by no means offers a Shakespeare without words. It is well informed about Elizabethan drama in general, and about the theatrical and critical history of Shakespeare's plays. Kozintsev's book is fairly representative of it, and has two representative defects. The first I shall mention here, the second in my summing up. The first is less a defect than a mark of the adversity under which all unsensational criticism of Shakespeare now suffers: it tells us nothing new. What it says about Shakespeare has been said in so many ways by so many people that it can no longer excite. It takes a genius equal to Shakepeare's to excite us with what we already know.

The point is that the Shakespeare who is Kozintsev's contemporary turns out to be pretty much the Shakespeare who was the contemporary of critical spokesmen from the seven-teenth through the nineteenth centuries. The Shakespeare who is Kott's contemporary would be unrecognizable to any of these spokesmen. Nevertheless, Kott's book, though pro-duced in Poland, is indubitably a Western document, wholly inspired by art and ideas prevalent on our side of the Iron Curtain. The thought gives one pause. In 1966 an anthology of Shakespearean criticism, written in English though pub-lished in Russia, was prefaced by R. M. Samarin, who de-scribed the Soviet Union as "a country in which Shakespeare has truly found a second home—a vast country, generous in love and gratitude."[7] Is there a chance that this "second home" will become the *only* home, indeed the refuge of the pre-Kottian Shakespeare? Before succumbing to panic, I must continue to examine the evidence. My next piece is not com-forting. At the Tenth International Shakespeare Conference, held at Stratford-on-Avon in 1963, Samarin was the Soviet delegate. He read a paper called "Our Closeness to Shake-speare." Its conclusion, addressed of course to East and West, was "Our closeness to Shakespeare brings us closer to each other. For this feeling of unity in the name of the great values of universal culture we have Shakespeare to thank."[8] At this same conference a Western delegate read a paper called "Shakespeare and the Temper of These Times." In it Samar-in's "great values of universal culture" figured under the dif-ferent and dampening label of "decorous moral and intel-lectual conformities."[9] After mentioning the possible values of "romantic nihilism" and its triumph in the theatre of the absurd, the delegate said, "perhaps the time is ripe for the

[7] *Shakespeare in the Soviet Union: A Collection of Articles,* comp. R. M. Samarin and A. Nikolyukin (Moscow, 1966), p. 14.

[8] *Shakespeare Survey,* vol. 16, ed. Allardyce Nicoll (Cambridge, 1963), p. 17.

[9] J. P. Brockbank, ibid., p. 34.

study of Shakespeare's pessimism." Actually the study had already been written and was just being launched on its great career.[10]

This delegate was not directly rebuking Samarin and his hopeful affirmations, or endorsing in full the idea of a pessimistic Shakespeare. He evidently belongs to the school of thinkers who see value in "romantic nihilism" because of the "value of extreme commitments" as a cure for our malaise. The idea seems to be that sacrilege implies the sacred, that only the damned can apprehend the glory of salvation, that assertion of human indignity may be a route to recovered dignity. One may question whether any "commitment" so sedentary as that of the literary critic may be called "extreme," and point out that there exists a still more "romantic" view of the value of modern nihilism:[11] if we could shuffle off entirely the restraints and obligations concomitant with "cultural values," we might return to that golden age of instinctual living when every day was a Dionysiac holiday. It is beyond my powers to evaluate or even quite comprehend these modernistic yearnings, but whether barbarism should be viewed as a mode of rejuvenation or as a boon itself is scarcely the point at issue. The real question is, what has all this to do with Shakespeare? My objection is solely to the statement that "perhaps the time is ripe for the study of Shakespeare's pessimism," presumably because it may have some doctrinal (or counterdoctrinal) utility. What this spokesman seems to be saying is that Shakespeare has had so many Pelagian critics that we should loose upon him a few Manicheans.

I fail to see how the time can ever be ripe for the "study" of the nonexistent, or how the plays can seem to us rewarding

[10] Kott's essays, published in Poland in 1961, had already been translated into French.

[11] Lionel Trilling, "On the Modern Element in Modern Literature," in *Varieties of Literary Experience,* ed. Stanley Burnshaw (New York, 1962).

in their wholeness if we are willing to throw them into the hopper to be shredded in ideological warfare. Even a suspicion of the gesture is damaging. I mentioned a second defect in Kozintsev's rival book. I cannot speak of it without first affirming that it and the kind of current Soviet criticism of Shakespeare which it represents seems to me more vital and humane than much of our own. I can say this without danger of having my passport lifted, and therein lies my point. The defect resides in the mere fact that the book comes from a state where public utterances must be officially sanctioned and therefore come under suspicion of conforming with official doctrine. Its author is obviously sincere, but we cannot accept comfortably what anyone says about anything unless he is free to say the opposite. The faults of Kozintsev's book are contingent faults. Kott's book has a contingent virtue—it exercises the right to be wrong. There can be little doubt that its vogue in Czechoslovakia stemmed largely from the fact that it suggested a means, in the theatre, of thumbing the nose at Big Brother. We can sympathize with the Czechs without endorsing Kott's view of *A Midsummer Night's Dream* as a study in bestiality. As advocates of freedom we need not love all our clients.

I return now to my starting point. What is the evidence that Shakespeare's plays are still living literature, in the sense that they can still be enjoyed spontaneously, without impulse either to emphasize or alter their ethical and religious orientation? Must we regretfully concede that the idea of a truly companionable Shakespeare is only a nostalgic dream? that "nothing gold can stay"? The evidence of his living quality is not supplied in our theatres. The present orthodoxy among Shakespearean directors is that the plays must be boldly reinterpreted so as to seem "relevant to our times." In practice this seems to mean that they must be falsified. The fact that the process of bold reinterpretation has failed to inaugurate a grand new era of Shakespearean production scarcely proves the directors wrong. The theatrical public which takes only a languid interest in Shakespeare modified might take no interest at all in Shakespeare unmodified.

The evidence of the viability of an uninvaded Shakespeare is not provided by current Shakespearean criticism, despite its mounting abundance. Some of this criticism is worthwhile, and certainly that which takes account of the words is better than that which does not, but with the first words of commentary a trace of doctrine filters in. I speak in a free society, but I am aware that my belief in "eternal verities" must appear as partisanship the moment I speak of the *meaning* of this play or that. To defend the validity of one's commentary by asserting that it is obvious and unoriginal invites a withering response: if it is obvious and unoriginal, it should also be unnecessary—better be original and wrong, on the remote chance of being at least amusing. The salient fact is that, except for the small portion which is simply descriptive and appreciative, Shakespearean commentary is now argumentative, and whether it defends old and obvious meanings or proposes new and esoteric ones, it relocates the plays in the realm of doctrine. In assuming that a spontaneous and innocent response is irrelevant or impossible, it bears no witness to the living quality of Shakespeare's art; rather it pays it elegiac tribute.

The best evidence for the survival of Shakespeare in our day is provided by those who rarely go the theatre and who rarely read criticism but who do read the plays. These readers are getting a Shakespeare with words, and with words wholly his own. Having said so much about Shakespeare without words, let me conclude with a few remarks about Shakespearean criticism without words. In the fundamental sense of judgment or evaluation, such criticism exists. If there were not a page of Soviet commentary, there would still be Soviet criticism. The presses of Russia cannot supply the demand for Shakespeare's works, in English or in translation. I do not mention the many theatrical productions because I do not know what they are like, and to a variable degree they may be projecting a "Shakespeare East." Those Russian readers, however, are on their own, and, in finding Shakespeare interesting and enjoyable, they are silently rendering the judgment we value most. And of course what they are enjoying is not necessarily a Shakespeare in exile. There are readers in the West for whom a "Shakespeare West" exists only in critical works which they have not read and in theatrical productions which they effortlessly refrain from seeing. Their number is incalculable, but even though too scattered to exercise much influence, they will probably still be around when the modish critic and director have joined their predecessors in oblivion. Mr. Samarin could have made his point without mentioning "the great values of universal culture." If people East and West are enjoying in common something so worthwhile as Shakespeare they are indeed brought "closer together." I wish we could leave that something alone.

Oddly enough, criticism without words is what Shakespeare himself wanted and received. His plays evoked almost no written commentary in their own time—but there was criticism. I began with mention of the Epilogue to *The Tempest*. Its prologue, if one existed, is lost, but we know what it would have said. Like the other prologues of the period it would have been a plea for courteous attention, a plea for silence. And as the play wove its spell, as the others had woven theirs, a judgment was passed in the Globe. It was expressed by silence, except for a few wordless sound effects— the murmur of lament, the burst of laughter, the sigh of relief, and finally the sound of applauding hands.

2 SHAKESPEARE AND THE PROFESSIONS

*T*HE modest plan of this lecture is to present some general observations about Shakespeare's knowledge of the learned professions and, more particularly, about his attitude toward professional men. Soldiers, statesmen, and monarchs stand in the foreground of most of his canvases, and about them cluster scores of attendant lords. For the moment I shall ask you to turn your eyes from these, and observe a few figures in the background or on the edges of the scene. Even these few have given rise to considerable speculation in the vast reaches of Shakespearean commentary. My familiarity with it is far from complete, but the sampling I have done has led to certain conclusions—fortified by the return which we must constantly make to Shakespeare's works themselves.

As everyone must know, lovers of Shakespeare love to claim him as their own, and tend to see in the mirror of his works, if not themselves, at least those things to which their loyalties attach. So far as I have been able to determine, the first attempt to claim Shakespeare for a profession other than the obvious one of actor and playwright came in 1790 in the Malone edition of the *Works*. Edmond Malone was a true scholar and an honest man, but he happened also to be a lawyer. It is not surprising that he concluded that the abundance of legal terms woven into the texture of the language of the plays has too great an "appearance of technical skill" to have come from a mere amateur. "I suspect," said Malone, "he was early initiated in at least the forms of law; and was

The first Fred S. Tupper Memorial Lecture of the George Washington University, delivered in Washington, D.C., April 2, 1965, and printed privately for the patrons.

employed while he yet remained at Stratford, in the office of some country attorney."[1] A lengthy footnote quotes a number of legal terms used with professional accuracy, and thus selectively assembled they seem to provide evidence of formal training. Once the case for such training had been stated, the supporting proof seemed to grow miraculously. In 1858 the first full-length book on Shakespeare's legal attainments was published. Its author, William L. Rushton, who happened also to be a lawyer, was convinced that Shakespeare was formally trained, and although his work is not dogmatic in tone, he incautiously titled it *Shakespeare a Lawyer.*[2]

We can imagine how a book of this kind would strike a man like Charles Dickens. Himself only slightly indebted to formal education, he knew that the creative artist absorbs information from the surrounding air and can write on the case of Jarndyce and Jarndyce (or Shylock *v.* Antonio) without having qualified for the bar. In a fall issue of his magazine, *Household Words,* appears a take-off of lawyer Rushton's book.[3] Hydropathy was much in vogue at the time, and posing as a hydropathist or "water-doctor," the writer claims Shakespeare as a member of his profession. "I need hardly tell you," he writes solemnly, "that in the very first play in our friend's works, The Tempest, is the story of a great water-cure worked in an exceedingly hard case by one Prospero." He goes on to speak of the salutary effects of a mere dream of water upon Clarence in *Richard III,* and of the rain therapy in *King Lear,* especially as the old king lay in the leaky hovel. "Compare this," he continues, "with Shakespeare's perception of malpractice in another case of madness, that of Ophelia, who instead of receiving a trickle on the head, died of com-

---

[1] *The Plays and Poems of William Shakespeare,* ed. Edmond Malone, 10 vols. (London, 1790), I, 307.

[2] William L. Rushton, *Shakespeare a Lawyer* (London, 1858).

[3] *Household Words,* Oct. 23, 1858, pp. 454–456.

plete submersion. 'Too much of water hadst thou, poor Ophelia.' Even I myself could not have drawn the distinction with more accuracy."

No one seemed perturbed by this offstage laughter, and in the very next year John Campbell, who was not only a lawyer but the Lord Chancellor of the realm, published a book on Shakespeare's "legal acquirements."[4] With a lordly disregard both of Dickens' plebeian journal and Rushton's recent book, Campbell marshalled the evidence once more. Although he refrained from passing a final verdict, the effect of his argument was to tighten the claim of the lawyers upon the poet. But the competitive instinct of a rival profession was now aroused. In 1860 appeared a book called *The Medical Knowledge of Shakespeare,* which takes respectful issue with Lord Campbell and his views. The author, an actual allopath, takes a less aggressive line than the fictitious hydropath of *Household Words,* but he firmly denies that Shakespeare's knowledge of medicine was only "casual" as compared to his knowledge of law. Shakespeare, says this good Dr. Bucknill, was "a diligent student of all medical knowledge existing in his time." He refrains from claiming for the poet a "formal connection" with the medical profession because of the difficulty of visualizing him in youth as "both a lawyer's clerk and a doctor's apprentice."[5]

Thus far the discussion, although a little absurd, had been moderate and even informative. Some of the subsequent discussion has remained that way, but by no means all. Scores of books and articles have appeared, demonstrating Shakespeare's competence not only in common law but in statutory law, property law, canon law, and various more recondite

[4] John, Lord Campbell, *Shakespeare's Legal Acquirements Considered* (London, 1859).

[5] John C. Bucknill, *The Medical Knowledge of Shakespeare* (London, 1860), p. 290.

branches. The Baconians soon fastened on the subject and claimed that England's Lord Chief Justice alone could have possessed such vast and expert knowledge, whereupon the defenders of Shakespeare's rights discovered that his legal knowledge was less vast and expert than they had at first supposed.[6] Much of the law in the plays, they pointed out, is "bad law." This brought rejoinders, not always from Baconians, that what might seem "bad law" to the dull eye of the common attorney could be discerned as "good law" by the bright eye of the true legal scholar. One need only sample this deluge of publication to learn that any kind of law has been "good law" in some time or place. With the whole world to choose from, Shakespeare could not go wrong.

Spokesmen for the medical profession have proved equally diligent. By 1873 a book had appeared on Shakespeare as a physician,[7] and scores of books and articles have followed, with titles ranging from *William Shakespeare M.D.* to "William Shakespeare, Syphilographer,"[8] demonstrating the poet's fine qualifications both as general practitioner and as specialist. We learn that Richard the Third's crippled arm may have been self-induced by a strawberry diet, and that Macbeth's symptoms were those of battle fatigue. The mere word "itch" in the lines has proved enough to excite the dermatologist, even though the itches of our ancestors were often produced

[6] F. E. Schelling points out that Sidney Lee had changed his opinion about Shakespeare's legal knowledge when he revised his biography of the poet; see *Shakespeare and Demi-Science* (Philadelphia, 1927), pp. 127–128.

[7] H. Aubert, *Shakespeare als Mediziner* (Rostak, 1873).

[8] H. B. Epstein, *William Shakespeare, M.D.* (Newark, 1932); W. E. Vest, "William Shakespeare, Syphilographer," *West Virginia Medical Journal,* 34 (1938), 130–137. (I have not consulted these works.) For the recent writings on Shakespeare's medical knowledge, see G. R. Smith, *A Classified Shakespeare Bibliography, 1936–1958* (University Park, Pa., 1963), pp. 98–99. More prodigious both in amount and content are the writings by the psychoanalysts; ibid., pp. 47–56.

by agents which the merest layman might identify. There are treatises on Shakespeare and Gynecology, Obstetrics, Pediatrics, Ophthalmology, Toxicology, Pharmacology, Anatomy, Surgery, Sanitation, and so on. There are two separate articles on "Shakespeare and the Ears, Nose, and Throat." All this sounds more ludicrous than it really is. Most of this printed matter appears in medical journals, with the innocent intention of sweetening the clinical air with a few quotations from the beloved poet. There is something engaging about the eagerness of the authors to have Shakespeare share their own intense interest in scabies, twinning, "laterality dominance," and the like. The physicians have been praised for their restraint, never having claimed that their revered Renaissance predecessor, Dr. William Harvey, was the true author of the plays even though the characters seem to have circulating blood.

We may ask what the teaching profession has been doing about drawing Shakespeare into its orbit, and must answer that its members have been strangely negligent, particularly so since teaching is the sole vocation outside the theatre with which Shakespeare can be associated on documentary grounds. John Aubrey, the seventeenth-century recorder of miscellaneous information, was told by the son of one of Shakespeare's fellow actors, Christopher Beeston, that the poet was "in his younger yeares a School-master in the Countrey."[9] Unlike the legends about deer poaching and the like, this report has a clear and good descent; and since it is not picturesque, exciting, or scandalous, there would have been small point in preserving it except for the fact that it was true. If a mere eighteenth-century guess that he had served a legal apprenticeship could translate Shakespeare into a lawyer, we may well wonder why a good seventeenth-century record that

[9] John Aubrey, *Brief Lives;* see E. K. Chambers, *William Shakespeare,* 2 vols. (Oxford, 1930), II, 254.

he served a teaching apprenticeship has not translated him into a fellow of Oxford or Cambridge. Certainly his works teem with supporting evidence. Every line displays his proficiency in the chief subject of the Renaissance curriculum, the art of communication.[10] He could have given advanced courses in declamation, rhetoric, and literature; and since he was the coiner of the words "critic" and "critical," we can even guess at his approach. Still there have been no books called "Professor William Shakespeare" or "William Shakespeare, Ph.D." and we can only conclude that teachers are an unacquisitive or listless race.

Before drawing any conclusions about Shakespeare's competence in the learned professions, we should recognize that the ease with which he exploited their language is part of a general phenomenon. The competing books about Shakespeare as a sailor, a soldier, and so on should serve as sufficient reminder. Perhaps the most convincing book of all would present Shakespeare as a gamekeeper, since he shows an uncanny familiarity with the sports of field and forest. Nevertheless, it is true that we are constantly struck by surprising items of information—legal, medical, linguistic—subtending the imagery of the plays. It is usually not of the kind that would be "looked up" for the particular occasion, since the occasion is often inappropriate. It is too often forgotten that Shakespeare's plays, although written in Elizabethan England, were not set in Elizabethan England. In nineteen of them the scene is the coastal lands and islands of the Mediterranean, often in ancient times. In one it is medieval Denmark, in one a decadent Vienna, in three a dateless France. The re-

[10] A book by J. P. Chesney, *Shakespeare as a Physician* (St. Louis, 1884), is organized like a medical textbook. One may compare with it a book not designed to prove Shakespeare a teacher of rhetoric, and yet approximating a manual on the subject: Sister Miriam Joseph, *Shakespeare's Use of the Arts of Language* (New York, 1947).

maining fourteen are indeed set in the British Isles, but in times ancient, medieval, or early Tudor. We make an exception of *The Merry Wives of Windsor,* even though Falstaff, its principal character, seems to have died on the eve of Agincourt in 1415, since, except for this detail, the setting is indubitably English and contemporary. But in all of the rest of the plays set in England the most "modern" episode is the birth of Queen Elizabeth, which occurred thirty years before Shakespeare himself was born. Under the circumstances any material in these plays reflecting *Elizabethan* life and learning is there in the form of seepage. It is not only incidental, but also inadvertent and anachronistic. Logically, it should not be there at all.

But, of course, it *is* there; and what this seems to mean is that Shakespeare was attuned to his environment. He responded to the life of his times sensitively and with relish. The human mind retains best those things which interest it most, and the astonishing retentiveness of Shakespeare's mind is the gauge of the width of his interests. It was a curiously extroverted mind, compared with those of the more seriously regarded writers of our own day, many of whom seem able to think of nothing except thinking and to write of nothing except writing. So far as the professions are concerned, I believe that we can come to one sound conclusion. The wealth of informed imagery and allusion relating to them does not prove that Shakespeare was formally trained in all or any one of them, but it does prove that he was just as much interested in professional activity as in political and martial activity. One would not have guessed this from his choice of story material —dictated, of course, by its theatrical viability as well as its interest to him personally—and so the discussions of his "knowledge," however eccentric at times, have not really been in vain.

The question which naturally follows is whether Shakespeare's interest in the professions was attended by respect. What did he think of the value of professional activity and of the character of professional men? A word of caution is necessary at this point. A character in a play is bound to take on the coloration of the context and to be shaped in conformity with the principle of decorum. Thus, in Shakespeare's time, it was less permissible to create a clownish king or general than to create a clownish doctor or teacher, and also less likely that commanding figures will appear in farcical plays. A teacher or doctor in a farce may well appear as a farcical teacher or doctor, whereas in a tragedy he would not have done so. We cannot determine from Shakespeare's comical or serious treatment of individual professional men just how seriously he regarded the professions they represent. Rather we must observe the limits he set upon the ridicule in the ridiculous portraits, and what form the seriousness took in the serious portraits. Only then may we penetrate to his underlying attitudes. What we discover is that Shakespeare's instinct was to set a limit to ridicule, and to respect what he apparently deemed to be the most fundamental tenet of each professional code.

I may illustrate the point by speaking briefly of his portraits of members of the working clergy. Technically, no Protestants should appear in the plays at all since the time and place of action is invariably Catholic when it is not pagan, but a scattering of parsons appear, and even a few Puritans. These may receive comic treatment, but unlike similar clergymen in the plays of Jonson and Middleton, they are never lampooned as frauds. Great fun is made of Nathaniel in *Love's Labor's Lost*, but this "foolish mild man" is finally described both as "honest" and "a marvellous good neighbor."[11] We catch only a

---

[11] *Love's Labor's Lost* v.ii.574–578. (All plays are cited in the Pelican edition.)

glimpse of Oliver Martext in *As You Like It.* His name must be a jibe at the Puritans, but he is not divested of dignity. After his rebuff by Jaques and Touchstone he lifts his chin stoutly: " 'Tis no matter. Ne'er a fantastical knave of them all shall flout me out of my calling."[12] This kind of qualifying touch is apt to be puzzling to the modern reader; and, of course, in the more heavy-handed kind of stage production, it is always crudely eradicated. When Malvolio, in far-off and Catholic Illyria, is called "a kind of Puritan," a distinction immediately follows: "The devil a Puritan that he is, or anything constantly but a time-pleaser."[13] By implication the Puritans, however lacking in geniality or bad for theatrical business, must be regarded as at least sincere. Jonson and Middleton never blurred their comic stereotypes with admissions so damaging.

Or consider Shakespeare's friars. Five appear in the plays: Laurence and John in *Romeo and Juliet,* Francis in *Much Ado about Nothing,* and Peter and Thomas in *Measure for Measure.* Three of them have New Testament names, all seem to wear "cowls" and to dwell in appropriate "cells" or religious "houses," but there the verisimilitude ends. These are most fictitious friars: it would be hard from the data supplied in the plays to deduce the rule or even the function of the Franciscan or other mendicant orders. In fact their chief function as here suggested is to dream up unlikely intrigues or to run errands in those dreamed up by others. But along with the general impression that friars live a clandestine life on the fringes of society, another is also conveyed—that friars are mild, kindly, and truly religious men. Now in the London where Shakespeare wrote, the former frater-hall of the Dominicans was serving as a commercial playhouse, and this

---

[12] *As You Like It* iii.iii.93–94.
[13] *Twelfth Night* ii.iii.134–135.

was considered by most Londoners as a distinct improvement over its former sinister use. Why then are Shakespeare's Laurence, John, Peter, Francis, Thomas, such "nice" men—much "nicer" really than the friars of Chaucer, whose London teemed with their kind? We may say that distance has lent enchantment, but this was not so in Elizabethan drama generally. Libelous representation of the old religious orders was common if not universal. It is conspicuous, for instance, in *The Troublesome Reign of King John;* and it is characteristic of Shakespeare that, when he came to rework this play, he expunged the scenes displaying corruption among the rank and file of the church although he granted no similar immunity to its upper hierarchical figures. All ties together to give us a reliable impression of a Shakespearean attitude. He could treat the working clergy as sometimes futile or comic, but he was disinclined to treat them, whether Catholic or Protestant, as vicious, corrupt, or negligent in their office. He seems to have felt that the one thing that a professed man of God must not be is a hypocrite.

In the case of teachers, I should guess that the unpardonable fault in Shakespeare's eyes was indifference. Pedantry in a teacher, or even aspiring ignorance, might be treated as laughable, but not a contempt for learning. It has been said that schoolmasters were the one class of men whom he could not bring himself to like,[14] but the evidence does not really sustain this judgment. It is true that schoolmasters are alluded to by his characters as impoverished and despised, as they were in fact in Elizabethan times (and often since), and it is also true that going to school is mentioned with distaste. We hear of

[14] J. Dover Wilson, "The Schoolmaster in Shakespeare's Plays," *Essays by Divers Hands Being the Transactions of the Royal Society of Literature of the United Kingdom,* New Series, 9, ed. J. Bailey (Oxford, 1930), 9–34.

> ... the whining schoolboy, with his satchel
> And shining morning face, creeping like snail
> Unwillingly to school ...[15]

and this is by no means the only passage evoking the idea of schoolgoing as durance vile. But we must remember that even the progressive movement has failed to plant in the human heart an abiding love of school, and that the Elizabethan schools were not progressive. They were places where Latin grammar was instilled by means of rote recitation and the rod in sessions of eight hours a day, six days a week, all months of the year. Unlike the patients of the doctors, whose methods were equally rigorous, the pupils of the schoolmasters survived to tell the tale, and it would have been impossible for Shakespeare to refer to the school memories of his audience as anything but traumatic.

The fact that the schoolmasters who appear in his plays are comic figures relates, of course, to the fact that they appear in farces. Under the circumstances it is remarkable that they do not appear as ogres—are not portrayed as cruel or cynical. Even the lamentable Pinch in *The Comedy of Errors,* described as a "pedant and a conjuror" (because of his command of Latin), is a dutiful man according to his lights. The lampoon of Holofernes in *Love's Labor's Lost* is hilariously funny precisely because of this schoolmaster's sublime sense of mission and absorption in his subject. He sees people as parts of speech—"A soul feminine saluteth us,"[16] he observes of Jaquenetta's greeting—; and he thinks of rank in terms of phonetics—"thou consonant,"[17] he calls little Moth, because consonants without vowels are nothing. He is a supercilious ass—there is no question of that—but he is also out-giving,

[15] *As You Like It* ii.vii.145–147.
Love's Labor's Lost iv.ii.77.
[17] Ibid., v.i.49.

and his pedantical ardor is winning. One would prefer to send one's child to Holofernes' charge-house on the top of the mountain than to Squeers' Dotheboys Hall, or even to more reputable schools one might name. What he learned would be somewhat strange, a bit on the precious side, but he would at least learn something, and might even be ignited by Holofernes' synthetic sparks.

Hugh Evans in *The Merry Wives of Windsor,* teaching Latin with a Welsh accent, is an appealing figure, timorously brave and full of moral feeling. He is the one Shakespearean schoolmaster whom we actually see teaching.[18] He uses a judicious mixture of threat and encouragement as he hears little William's declensions: "hig, hag, hog . . . horum, harum, horum." When Mistress Quickly protests that the child should not be exposed to such nasty words as "horum" or, indeed, to the genitive case at all, master Evans speaks for all poor teachers who have been harassed by unqualified censors— "For shame, 'oman . . . art thou lunatics?" He threatens William with the rod when he trips on "qui, quae, quod," but what he actually does is to send him off to share in a recess— "Go your ways and play, go."

Elizabethan law courts, like grammar schools, were not calculated to leave fragrant memories and evoke images of delight. Shakespeare's high regard for Law, spelled with a capital letter, is a commonplace of commentary; but its day-to-day proceedings and practitioners must have seemed to him, as to everyone else, less lovely and majestic than the cause they presumably served. Hamlet laments the "law's delay" and alludes to the lawyer's "tricks" and "quiddities."[19] Jaques speaks of the lawyer's peculiar aberration as "politic"[20] (meaning in this context "devious"), and when Queen Mab's

[18] *Merry Wives of Windsor* iv.i.
[19] *Hamlet* iii.i.72; v.i.93–94.
[20] *As You Like It* iv.i.13.

35

tiny train passes over the fingers of the sleeping lawyer, he dreams of "fees."[21] In a word, the language of the plays often reflects those irritations which are a feature of universal experience. But this kind of reference is not overabundant, and our general impression is that Shakespeare viewed the legal processes, so ubiquitous in his life and times, without illusion but also without disgust. They had to be lived with, like the rain which raineth every day.

When we try to appraise his attitude to members of the profession, we are met by a curiosity. Court scenes and legalistic entanglements abound in the plays, but there are no practicing attorneys. Among Shakespeare's more than seven hundred characters only one is explicitly tagged as lawyer—an almost invisible character in I *Henry VI.* We never see a lawyer consulting with a client, transacting his business, or pleading his case. Even Shylock, who sorely needs one, appears in court without a lawyer. Portia posing as Dr. Bellario is the nearest we come to a portrait of a member of the profession in action. Her success in court (if not her indifference to a monetary fee) must be credited in part to the absent Paduan; his were the acute legal brains and hers the eloquence. In the hearing of Brabantio *v.* Othello, each of the principals pleads his own case, and this is entirely typical: we think of the "trial" of Hermione in *The Winter's Tale,* and of the several "trials" in *Measure for Measure.* Perhaps Shakespeare, with his own matchless qualifications to practice, excludes rival lawyers as superfluous.

On the other hand, there are judges and justices—some of them *ex officio,* like the several presiding dukes, others by virtue of their formal preparation. The latter vary in type from the Lord Chief Justice who is Falstaff's nemesis, to Justice Shallow, whom Falstaff mulcts. Justice Shallow has studied

---

[21] *Romeo and Juliet* i.iv.73.

law at Lincoln's Inn and knows that "A friend i' th' court is better than a penny in purse," but it is his serving man Davy who applies the principle—on behalf of his friend Visor: "I grant your worship that he is a knave, sir, but yet God forbid, sir, but a knave should have some countenance at his friend's request. An honest man, sir, is able to speak for himself."[22] This seems reasonable to Justice Shallow, but even his dim light keeps the laws of the realm faintly legible: he tries to administer the impressment act honestly and to send the King the best recruits. Shakespeare's justices, and even his constables, like Dogberry, try to use good judgment, although not with complete success, and his judges try to be just. The unjust judge Angelo in *Measure for Measure* is the exception that proves the rule; and he is counterpoised by the just judge Escalus, whose patience and fairness are exemplary as he copes with the vice of a demoralized Vienna.

It is apparent that Shakespeare was reluctant to show members of the legal professions as perverters of the law—using it as mere instrument of gain or aggression. The fact that he portrays no practicing lawyers at all may seem to reduce the significance of the fact that he portrays no shysters. On the other hand, the opportunity was there and a number of his contemporaries seized it. Their freedom underscores his restraint. Lawyers in claiming Shakespeare as their own have been willing to forgive his failure to give members of their profession work. The practice of the law is more generously treated by him than by almost any other major English writer.

The medical profession has even more reason to feel grateful. Except in Shakespeare, the portrait of the doctor in Elizabethan drama is prevailingly hostile. Even the tolerant Thomas Dekker called medicine the "Ars Homicidiorum"[23] and viewed its practitioners as a menace. He was not far

[22] *2 Henry IV* v. i. 27–28, 37–40.
[23] Thomas Dekker, *The Guls Hornbook*.

wrong. With its leechings, cuppings, bleedings, and violent purgings, and its armament of fantastic potions, medical practice at the time was an ally of disease. An energetic and conscientious lawyer was then as useful to a client in trouble as at any time before or since, but the more energetic and conscientious the doctor, the greater the danger to the patient. One's chance of recovery was greater, then and for some generations to come, if he could not afford a doctor. It is a matter of peculiar interest, therefore, that Shakespeare's doctors, unlike those of fact and fiction in his times, are shown not only as exemplary in their personal characters, but as successful in working cures.

It has been suggested that Shakespeare's apparent esteem for the profession stems from his esteem for his son-in-law, Dr. John Hall, and the possibility is worth a glance. The earlier plays portray only one physician, the fiery Frenchman Caius, who in *The Merry Wives of Windsor* is the mother's unsuccessful candidate for the hand of "sweet Ann Page." We do not see Dr. Caius practicing medicine, but only displaying his comical ineligibility as a bridegroom. Dr. Hall almost certainly arrived in Stratford after Shakespeare had written his village farce, and unlike Dr. Caius, he must have seemed eligible indeed for the hand of any unattached maiden. He was a gentleman born, a man of substance, a graduate of Cambridge, and a licentiate of the College of Physicians, destined to win a fine reputation both for piety and for devotion to his work. He was thirty-two, eleven years younger than his father-in-law, when his marriage to Susanna Shakespeare occurred in June 1607. Susanna was then twenty-four, and already a spinster by the standards of the day. A daughter, Elizabeth, born to the couple in 1608, was Shakespeare's only grandchild at the time of his death, and his will reveals how his hopes for a lasting posterity were linked to this little girl.

We must concede that there is good reason to suppose that he felt esteem and even gratitude to Dr. John Hall. His flattering portraits of doctors occur in plays written from 1602 onwards, some of them certainly and all of them possibly after he had come to know this admirable man. The fact may be significant or it may be a mere coincidence. There is a distinct possibility that the doctors in his dramatis personae would have appeared pretty much as they are had the playwright had no acquaintance or family connection with a member of the medical profession, since his attitude toward it is no different in essentials from his attitude toward the professions in general.

In *All's Well That Ends Well* we hear of Dr. Gerard de Narbon, "whose skill was almost as great as his honesty; had it stretched so far, would have made nature immortal."[24] The king of France remembers him as a paragon, and one of his remedies, posthumously administered by his daughter Helena, saves the king's life. In *Pericles* the physician Cerimon is thus addressed:

> Your honor has through Ephesus poured forth
> Your charity, and hundreds call themselves
> Your creatures, who by you have been restored;
> And not your knowledge, your personal pain, but even
> Your purse, still open, hath built Lord Cerimon
> Such strong renown as time shall never raze.[25]

In snatching Thaisa from death when her cold body is tossed upon the shores of Ephesus, Cerimon administers one of his "blest infusions." Like Narbon's lifesaving remedy, it remains tactfully undescribed, but we can surely approve of the rest of the treatment—warmth, dry linens, and aftercare: "And

---

[24] *All's Well That Ends Well* I.i.17-18.
[25] *Pericles* III.ii.43-48.

Aesculapius guide us!" In *Cymbeline* the physician Cornelius thwarts the murderous Queen by supplying her only an opiate when she asks for poison. Cornelius protests even against her pretext for wanting the latter, in order to conduct experiments on animals:

> Your Highness
> Shall from this practice but make hard your heart.[26]

Even more impressive are the physicians in *King Lear* and *Macbeth*. In preparing to treat the frenzy of Lear, the nameless doctor says,

> Our foster nurse of nature is repose,
> The which he lacks. That to provoke in him
> Are many simples operative, whose power
> Will close the eye of anguish.[27]

He prescribes nothing further than a sedative, fresh garments, music, and wisest remedy of all, the attendance of Cordelia at his side. The treatment deserved its success. Dr. Hall's casebook has recently been edited, and we are able to satisfy our curiosity about what Shakespeare's son-in-law might have prescribed in a similar situation. Although not called upon to treat King Lear, aged four score and upwards, he was called upon to treat one Master Kempson, aged three score and "oppressed with Melancholy, and a Feaver with extraordinary heat."[28] He applied to the soles of the patient's feet "Radishes sliced besprinkled with Vinegar and Salt" to draw back the "Vapours" which caused "starting and fear." This was his mildest prescription. Leeches were applied, and enemas, physics, and emetics administered, all composed of frighten-

[26] *Cymbeline* I.v.23–24.

[27] *King Lear* IV.iv.12–15.

[28] Harriet Joseph, *Shakespeare's Son-in-law: John Hall, Man and Physician* (Hamden, Conn., Shoe String, 1964), pp. 26–27.

ing ingredients. We are reminded of lines in the non-Shake-spearean part of *Pericles:*

> Thou speak'st like a physician, Helicanus,
> That ministers a potion unto me
> That thou would'st tremble to receive thyself.[29]

One of these potions was an "Emetick Infusion" containing "oxymel of Squils," which produced, as the case book faithfully records, "four Vomits and nine Stools." Master Kempson recovered and, as Dr. Hart happily notes, "lived for many years." It was, as he says and we can agree, "beyond all expectation."

In *Macbeth,* the doctor is called upon to treat perturbations less violent than Lear's but also less remediable. He detects a sickness of the soul, and says, "This disease is beyond my practice."[30] We owe to Professor Kocher the note that this dilemma reflects an Elizabethan controversy.[31] Physicians were suspected of being atheistic empirics, inclined to believe that even the pricks of conscience could be treated as physical symptoms. It was a prophetic issue: our psychiatric science has not yet defined for us the precise boundary between sick sense of guilt and wholesome sense of guiltiness, and how we can cure the one without killing the other. Shakespeare's doctor is religiously orthodox when he refrains from prescribing for Lady Macbeth: "More needs she the divine than the physician." He is consistent when addressed by Macbeth:

> Canst thou not minister to a mind diseased,
> Pluck from the memory a rooted sorrow,
> Raze out the written troubles of the brain,
> And with some sweet oblivious antidote

[29] *Pericles* i.ii.67–69.

[30] *Macbeth* v.i.54.

[31] Paul Kocher, "Lady Macbeth and the Doctor," *Shakespeare Quarterly,* 5 (1954), 341–349.

> Cleanse the stuffed bosom of that perilous stuff
> Which weighs upon the heart?[32]

This sounds wonderfully modern, like a description of neurotic symptoms, but the doctor responds as to a confession: "Therein the patient must minister to himself."

Nevertheless this Scotch practitioner resembles in an important particular the Briton who treats the more sinned against than sinning Lear. He is solicitous for the welfare of Lady Macbeth, even though horrified by his guess at the cause of her condition. He feels no impulse to expose her, and does all that he can do:

> God, God, forgive us all! Look after her;
> Remove from her the means of all annoyance,
> And still keep eyes upon her.[33]

True, he would like to be far from Dunsinane—"Profit again should hardly draw me here"—but while there in attendance, he remains true to his professional as well as his religious code.

If we omit the word "learned" and accept as "professional" all those nonmenial occupations in which members of the middle class serve society, we find that the group so occupied in Shakespeare's plays—the shipmasters, stewards, women-in-waiting, prison officials, and the like—yields his highest percentage of decent characters, unheroic though they may be. Surprisingly enough, Shakespeare's jailors are as conscientious and humane as his physicians, and the steward Flavius is the one truly fine character in the play where he appears. We may question, I think, the common assumption that Shakespeare's social bias was aristocratic, but that is scarcely the point. Whatever his social bias, the idea of human service on the nonspectacular plane held considerable appeal for him. And he

[32] *Macbeth* v.iii.40–45.
[33] Ibid., v.i.70–72.

was averse to attacking institutions, even those so vulnerable as the College of Physicians. Since its future was bright although its present was gloomy, we can scarcely complain that he viewed it in terms of its ideals rather than its accomplishments. He served the long-range truth better than did the satiric realists, although the latter stuck closer to the facts.

I should like to conclude with mention of a somewhat more imposing representative of Professor Tupper's profession, and my own, than Holofernes and Hugh Evans. When I was honored with the invitation to give this lecture, the accompanying tribute to Professor Tupper described him as a "man of quiet dignity who combined an avid enthusiasm for literature with an active interest in the world about him." Upon asking myself to what character in Shakespeare these words would best apply, the answer came at once—to Prospero in *The Tempest.* Prospero's "avid enthusiasm for literature" lost him his dukedom. The "liberal arts," he says, were "all my study" and "my library/Was dukedom large enough."[34] But when exiled to his island, he left his ivory tower. He still had his beloved books, and he now applied them in his "active interest in the world about him." Although there were only two youngsters on the island, Caliban and Miranda, he promptly opened a school. Since he himself describes himself as "schoolmaster," teachers, I think, have as much right to claim him for their profession as the physicians have to claim Cerimon, who was also a lordly amateur.

Prospero's score as teacher was one failure and one success. The dropout Caliban snarls at his old master: "You taught me language, and my profit on't/Is, I know how to curse."[35] It is a frightening utterance—not without present-day relevance. Neither is Caliban's morose and pathetic conception of "free-

---

[34] *The Tempest* I.ii.73–74, 109–110.
[35] Ibid., I.ii.363–364.

dom"—freedom to be beastly rather than human. But Prospero's graduate, Miranda, justifies his pedagogical pride:

> . . . here
> Have I, thy schoolmaster, made thee more profit
> Than other princess can, that have more time
> For vainer hours, and tutors not so careful.[36]

Miranda is both cultivated and full of hope:

> How beauteous mankind is! O brave new world
> That has such people in't![37]

This, too, is not without present-day relevance. Miranda is
the idealistic graduate who, by thinking of mankind as better
than it is, may help to make it so. A teacher who produces
one Miranda may consider his career a success. I am sure that
Professor Tupper's score was better than that. This lecture
series stands as evidence that he was able to create gratitude
—one of the most precious virtues.

Finally I should like to say that Shakespeare's teaching
career was a success. It is unfashionable to speak of literary
art as a form of teaching, but it can be so in one of its effects.
The members of all professions like to think of Shakespeare
as their own because he expressed their aspirations. All who
profess humanity have learned something in Shakespeare's
school.

[36] Ibid., i.ii.171–174.
[37] Ibid., v.i.183–184.

3 MARLOWE DISINTERRED

*T*HE season's candidate as the "real" Shakespeare is Marlowe of the mighty line. To picture this turbulent poet in the guise of the gentle bard is to recoil like Little Red Riding Hood: "Why, grandma, what big teeth you have!" Did Marlowe, like reaped clover, wither and grow sweet? Or was the kindly Shakespearean visage really a savagely ironic mask? The case for the "gentle" Marlowe may be summed up in a sentence. He was not slain in 1593, as the records falsely attest, but was whisked out of sight by his compromised lover, Sir Francis Walsingham, and lived on incognito to write the plays of Shakespeare—as, let us say, El Greco might have lived on to paint the canvases of Velásquez. The argument is unencumbered by anything resembling supporting evidence or critical perception. It is a bright idea springing from the head of a Long Island journalist, who tells us that for nearly two decades he has "roamed through churchyards," "crawled into dusty tombs," and patiently investigated "ancient houses, decaying churches, and old universities," while "clues came thick and fast" and the load of his inquiries seemed often a "burden too heavy to bear." Clearly these decades were spent in leaving no cliché unturned.

At least Marlowe was a true poet, and a resuscitated corpse seems little less plausible than the other "real" Shakespeares —for instance the poetic nun, Anne Whately, who never existed at all except as a clerical error in one of the Shakespearean documents, yet was solemnly pronounced the true author of the plays in a book by one William Ross. The trouble

This essay appeared in the *New York Times Book Review,* June 12, 1955, after the publication of *The Man Who Was Shakespeare* by Calvin Hoffman.

with Marlowe is not that so many of the plays claimed as his were written after his death—the Earl of Oxford shares this handicap—but that he was a mere commoner whereas our times must have a lord.

A sketch of the background of this queer business should prove more useful than refutation of the case of a sure loser like Marlowe. Refutation is futile anyway. Odd notions are dignified by serious dispute, and faddists win followers the moment they flush out adversaries. Scholars have been dropping into this trap for years, and doubts about Shakespeare's identity derive partly from their plaintive insistence that he wrote his plays. More than two score candidates have been promoted as the "real" Shakespeare. One might say that their claims cancel out, but their claims were all nil in the first place, without need of this or any other form of cancellation, and the actual effect of the unilateral series of refutations has been almost to cancel out Shakespeare. Whoever the plaintiff, he is always the defendant, and no reputation could survive intact these constant appearances in the dock. Each "case" has eased the way for the next, until the one thing most people now think they know about Shakespeare is that he may have been someone else.

To understand the implications of the authorship controversy one must first dismiss the notion that it has a rational basis. We have more reliably documented information about Shakespeare than about Aeschylus, Sophocles, Euripides, Aristophanes, Plautus, Terence, all medieval English playwrights combined, and all but a few of those of the Renaissance. Midway in his career he was the leading writer for one of the three London popular theatrical troupes. The leading writers for the other two were Thomas Dekker and Thomas Heywood, who between them wrote over three hundred plays, a number of which were printed, along with copious nondramatic works complete with dedicatory epistles. Yet all that is known of Heywood's birth, parentage, marriage, and offspring is purely conjectural, and nothing is known of Dekker's. No playwright's life was then written up, and the most remarkable thing about Shakespeare's is that our record of it is as full as it is.

So also with his creative activity. The identity of theatre writers then, like the identity of cinema and television writers now, was a matter of public indifference. Of the millions who now watch Bob Hope and Jack Benny how many can name their "writers"? The question in Shakespeare's time would have been, who can name the writers for Ed Alleyn and Dick Burbage? No "front" was needed for anyone who wished covertly to feed the virtually anonymous torrent of stage pieces. The most popular single play of the era, *The Spanish Tragedy,* went through ten editions without indication of author, and it is only a single casual allusion that lets us now assign it to the scrivener's son, Thomas Kyd. Marlowe's claim to his own famous *Tamburlaine* is based on circumstantial evidence; no one troubled to put his name on the title page. Again Shakespeare is exceptional, in that his superiority was so well recognized among readers that the record of his authorship is uniquely full. He was by no means the most prolific playwright of the time, but his is the most constantly recurring name on title pages and in the Stationers' Register.

His social background was precisely what literary historians would surmise even if there were no confirmation. The popular playwrights as a class were humbly born, with the standing of the Shakespeare family somewhat above the average. In fact most of the fine literary art of the Renaissance (and since) emanated from the emergent middle classes. Chaucer was the son of a vintner, Spenser the son of a linen draper, Marlowe the son of a shoemaker, Donne the son of an ironmonger, Milton the son of a scrivener, and so it goes. Some of the sires were more prosperous than others, but few indeed were aristocrats. To be the son of a Stratford glovemaker was not poetically disabling. A glance toward the Continent reveals as the peak figures Rabelais, Cervantes, and Molière—all three humbly derived. Those craving association of noble birth with noble works have been so troubled by the case of Cervantes that the Baconians have come to their aid with the announcement that Sir Francis was the author of *Don Quixote* as well as *Hamlet.*

Finally, it must be pointed out that Shakespeare's education was also entirely typical. Most of the popular writers were products of the Latin grammar schools, few of them as good as Stratford's. When we cannot find their names in the registers, it is because we cannot find the registers, and Shakespeare is but one of many whose attendance is a matter of reasonable inference. Of over twenty playwrights who emerged with Shakespeare in the 1590's only three or four had proceeded further than grammar school. The learned Ben Jonson was self-taught after his Westminister grammar school days during a youth spent bricklaying, soldiering, and acting. George Chapman became the famed translator of Homer, and Michael Drayton the purveyor of a vast body of native history, topography, and folklore without benefit of advanced formal education. (With a touching faith in the efficacy of a college degree, Marlowe's advocate points with pride to his candidate's M.A.)

If we look then for a basis of doubt about Shakespeare's authorship, some small piece of evidence, however exaggerated, we find no basis, no evidence, no point of departure whatever. His claim to his writings is of the same kind and degree of validity as Hemingway's claim to his, and although there is a mathematical chance that *The Old Man and the Sea* was written by Einstein or the Duke of Windsor, it seems unworth a gamble at any odds. Neither about Shakespeare nor about any of his contemporaries is there a hint of the kind of hoax that must be postulated, and the conditions of authorship were such as to render one even less reasonable then than now. "Ghost-writing" has now become common, but the conditions are fairly predictable: generals, statesmen, and other celebrities do not write the pieces signed by our journalists. The scores of elaborate "cases" against Shakespeare, presented in hundreds of thick treatises, may be reduced to the following statement: "The plays are learned and aristocratic, and must therefore have been written by a scholar like Bacon or an aristocrat like Oxford, not by an ignorant peasant like Shakespeare." The charm of the statement is that it is equally false in all its parts.

Shakespeare's plays are not *learned*. They were viewed as the reverse in their own day and for a century afterward. For Jonson, Shakespeare "wanted art" (that is, the kind of intellectual training commemorated in the term "Bachelor of Arts"); for Milton he was "fancy's Child"; for Dryden he was "naturally" learned—"he needed not the spectacles of books." The myth of his vast learning arose in the eighteenth century when his mounting prestige made him seem a desirable member of any man's club and the scholars got in first with their bid—not the true scholars like Samuel Johnson and Edmond Malone, but the pseudoscholars like Charles Gildon or the myopic ones like John Upton. By claiming for Shakespeare all kinds of recondite knowledge they displayed their own until the myth exploded of absurdity. It was, for instance, finally demonstrated that Shakespeare's Roman plays derived from a popular translation of Plutarch, abiding even by its misprints of place names, as compared with Jonson's *Sejanus* and *Catiline,* which derived from a fund of classical reading fortified by special research. It is beside the point that Shakespeare succeeds better than Jonson in seeming to recreate ancient Rome—we are not speaking of creative imagination or intuition. So far as book learning is concerned, the dispute of the eighteenth century led finally to an endorsement of the earlier view, that Shakespeare was reasonably well read but was far from being a scholar, and the impulse to bid him in passed to other professions and sects. He has since been claimed by all, not excluding the society of sexual deviants. Lawyers have been especially diligent, and a fair number of physicians have even conferred upon him the diseases in which they specialize.

When the myth of learning was abandoned by the scholars, it passed on to the less literate public, and we can understand the reasons why. The plays *looked* learned. Their classical allusions were imposing to the many whose Latin was considerably less than that provided by the Renaissance grammar schools, and their poetic idiom seemed increasingly esoteric as the age to which it was native receded. Moreover the day of idolatry had dawned. Idolatry may be defined as veneration of an object without reference to its true nature or value. In nonprimitive societies it often takes the form of adulation by hearsay and mass suggestion. Shakespeare was being edited and discussed by learned men, and Shakespeare was venerated as learning was venerated. The situation favored idolatrous fusion, the germination of a cult.

In the late eighteenth and early nineteenth centuries there were underground rumors that the plays had been written by no mere actor but by the most learned man of their time. In the mid-nineteenth century several books on the subject appeared, whereupon the floodgates opened. The hundreds of Baconian treatises and the thousands of Baconian converts must be referred in part to the *Zeitgeist*. The late nineteenth century was peculiarly linked to the image of Sir Francis Bacon, apostle of material progress and composer of moral maxims. Surely a predisposing sentiment, an underlying emotion, was working in favor of this particular candidate at this particular time. The rise and fall of the Baconian cult should alert us to the implications of its successor. That rival candidates would appear might be taken for granted; the interesting question is why the favored candidate at the present time should be archetypal aristocrat rather than archetypal man of learning.

Shakespeare's plays are even less *aristocratic* than learned. They are "noble" in a metaphoric sense but no other, as may readily be determined by comparing them with contemporary plays written by authentic noblesse such as the Earl of Stirling, the Countess Pembroke, Lord Brooke, and others— neoclassical works of uniformly dignified sobriety. When aristocrats felt the impulse to write drama, they wrote in the sanctioned mode, and would no more have contented themselves with Shakespeare's mode than with his horse, rapier, and doublet. Of course Shakespeare's plays feature kings and noblemen—they may *look* aristocratic—but the determining factor is that for the many who know them only by hearsay they operate only as a detached symbol of value. Let the aristocrat succeed the scholar as linked object of veneration and we get a modified cult, a fusion of altered ingredients.

In 1891 the Earl of Derby was publicly nominated as the "real" Shakespeare, in 1905 the Earls of Rutland and Essex, and in 1920 the Earl of Oxford. There have also been a countess, several barons, and sundry knights. If one asks why no dukes, the answer is simple—no dukes are available in Elizabethan times: the old queen was too canny to install anyone in a rank so near her throne. If a nobleman is needed, the Earl of Oxford is about the best one can find. Seventeenth in descent in the de Vere line, he was almost a museum piece among the "new men" who dominated the court of Elizabeth. He was also bigoted, humorless, unstable, and morally obtuse, but perhaps this is beside the point. The book in which Oxford was nominated, *"Shakespeare" Identified,* by J. T.

Looney, is the cleverest of its kind but is completely true to type. After denigrating Shakespeare's family and town with all their ways, it applies the Conan Doyle technique of inverted induction, but without Doyle's charming consciousness of charlatanry. When the mud spatter on the trouser cuff leads Holmes to the inspired conclusion that his visitor must have sat at the side of his hansom cab instead of in the center, and so must have left a companion sitting in it down there on Baker Street, Doyle knew that he was giving Holmes backstage assistance. He knew that although the mud spatter might be explained in less relevant ways, Watson (and the reader) would accept its validity as a clue the moment the companion was produced. "Holmes, this is marvelous!"

Just so is the Earl of Oxford *produced*. Was he not, as the author of these plays must have been, familiar with Italy, with music, with falconry, with this and with that, above all with *aristocratic ways!* By this method it would be boringly easy to prove that the plays were written by Winston Churchill. All such books are riddled with factual distortions, such as the casual reader is ill equipped to detect, but one would suppose that anyone literate enough to be interested could detect the elementary non sequitur not to mention critical naïveté.

The last thin line of Baconians are desperately asserting that their candidate was of *royal* blood, but nothing—and certainly not poor Marlowe's claims—will stem the Oxfordian groundswell. Societies have been organized, periodicals launched, and an amazing number of people heard sagely to remark that "there must be something in it." What underlying emotion, what predisposing sentiment, in such presumed bulwarks of democracy as England and America is making it easier to associate any kind of distinction with a lord than a commoner is a problem for the social historian. Especially depressing is the debonair cant of the neutralists—

those who say that so long as we have the plays it does not matter who wrote them. It does matter. The truth always matters, and the habit of playing games with it is contagious. The Holmes technique is increasingly imitated and admired in fields of literary inquiry once marked by a quiet reliability. It is hard to be amused by the pastime of robbing the dead, or by the debasement of works of art into grab bags of alleged clues, cryptograms, and petty topicalities. Under such erosion what happens to our precious heritage? Casting doubt upon the genesis of the plays is halfway to casting doubt upon their existence, or at least their claim on our attention. By similar ruses we find protection from the Sermon on the Mount. The great things are encysted, like lesions in the comfortable tissue of mediocrity.

The most charitable thing one may say about the "authorship controversy" is that it attests to a belief that one *ought* to be interested in literature. Discussing authors is less fatiguing than reading books. Among my acquaintances is an elderly lady who gently ignores my adherence to the man from Stratford because her own enlightenment came late. She asked me recently if I did not consider utterly ridiculous the theory that Marlowe wrote Oxford's plays. After conceding that I did, I maliciously asked which of milord's plays she had most recently been reading. Her innocent evasions made me feel most unkind.

4 SHAKESPEARE INTERRED?

*T*HE proposal that Marlowe wrote Shakespeare's plays won notice in journals as various as *Coronet* and *Columbia*. It was reported in small local newspapers and in *Life* and *Time*. The *New York Times* deemed it news fit to print on no less than twelve occasions, once on the front page. I myself was nearly catapulted into fame when my comments on the proposal were published, no doubt because a positive position of any kind seems novel in a temporizing age. I was asked to extend my remarks in a book (once), in magazine articles (twice), on radio or television (four times), and in lectures (nine). In several instances the platform appearances were to be as participant in a debate, one under the auspices of the *Harvard Law Review,* whose services to the nation have been less conspicuous in Shakespearean studies than in other fields of inquiry. In declining these offers I once or twice mentioned, experimentally, that I might be persuaded to offer a few remarks on the plays as literature. The suggestion met with the chill response which its irrelevance deserved.

True, everyone loves a mystery, but the fact scarcely explains the popular interest in attacks on Shakespeare's authorship. We must still ask why this particular mystery was so belatedly hatched, and why it involves Shakespeare rather than some other author, say Dante, or Dickens, or P. G. Wodehouse. A hint of the reason may appear in the anti-Shakespearean treatises themselves. In the line of duty I have read more of these than I like to recall, and I have noticed a curious thing about them. The writers never say anything

Adapted from "The Shakespeare Boom?" in the "Books and Men" section of the *Atlantic*, October 1956.

witty or wise, or even critically explicit, about the plays them-selves, whoever the proposed author. They assemble the usual superlatives of praise, but only in the most dutiful way, and it soon becomes evident that the plays which are so transparent to them as assorted clues and cryptograms are quite opaque as works of art. These tireless sleuths seem as impervious to the moral and emotional thrust of the plays as to the idea of Shakespeare as their author. The "block" is duplicated among the converts. Anyone who has sat in on a Baconian or Oxfordian meeting, or even listened to informal conver-sations among the faithful, can attest to the same phenomenon, that a kind of vacuum exists where the plays ought to be. These seem to have had no artistic impact, aroused no feeling, indeed won no response whatever except the intense con-viction that Shakespeare did not write them.

What this oddity suggests is that even the milder form of skepticism prevalent among the noncommitted, the wide-spread doubts about Shakespeare's reality, may be related to a widespread failure to experience the plays themselves as a reality. Perhaps Shakespeare is becoming a phantom author because his are becoming phantom plays, encountered only in the form of persistent rumor. If his works prove evasive, so must he, with his spectral identity assuming any shape sug-gested, that of Bacon, Oxford, Marlowe, or the Princess Poca-hontas (who must surely have sought *some* way of occupy-ing her time during her sojourn in London). I rarely dine out without having a lady at my side or a gentleman across the table ask me to resolve in a few telling words nagging doubts about Shakespeare's claim. There is something touch-ing about this conversational gambit, kindly deferring to my presumed interests at the same time that it displays the speaker's cultural concern, but I must regretfully report that those who employ it never seem very familiar with the works whose origin so deeply troubles them. The plain truth is that the people who actually read them tend to take their Shakespearean origin for granted.

It amounts to a general principle that a writer seems real to us in proportion to the reality of the impression conveyed by his writing. I once conferred with the co-producers of a quality television series, both talented, and in certain areas quite literate. If I had thrown out the suggestion that perhaps Gogarty had written the works of Joyce, or Pound the works of Eliot, they would have exchanged the nervous glances of sane men in the presence of lunacy. Yet presently came the familiar query, in slightly refined form: Just how can we be sure that the Shakespeare of Stratford was the Shakespeare of the London stage? When I mentioned the links provided by items in the Stratford will and in the prefatory material of the First Folio, they greeted the information with the deference due the fruits of strenuous research; yet it was certainly available in the elementary handbook or editions they had used as undergraduates. When the discussion turned to the plays, both deprecated their ignorance. They were not exaggerating. A secondary student in France knowing as little of the plays of Corneille, or one in Germany knowing as little of those of Goethe, would have felt humiliated.

Now why should this be so? Why is it that the body of writing conceded to be the best in English should have impinged on the consciousness of only a small minority of the multitudes exposed to it in schools and colleges? The fact when admitted is often blamed on the ineptitude of English teachers, as if Shakespeare's works were a dose which should be more skillfully administered. It may be true that teachers sometimes communicate only their own bemusement, but to be known, a writer must at least be met, and there would be even fewer to whom Shakespeare is a reality were it not for scholastic requirements. The true reason may be that a poet is a reality to a people only when he is moving its heart, clearing its vision, shaping its aspirations.

Shakespeare was this kind of reality in the English-speaking world during most of the nineteenth century. It is hard to imagine what its imaginative life would have been without him. Reading Shakespeare was the largest single instrumentality in compensating for the scanty formal schooling, indeed the cultural deprivation, of such writers as Keats and Dickens. When the latter as "David Copperfield" reads Shakespeare to Dora in the quixotic endeavor to "improve her mind," he is telling us something we could deduce for ourselves from the myriad of Shakespearean allusions and turns of phrase worked into the texture of his prose. Many in his great popular audience had themselves turned to Shakespeare in their efforts at self-education. Shakespeare was equally meaningful in America. That the Bible and Shakespeare reached the frontier just behind the rifle and the axe is more than a pious fancy. His plays were performed more often than any others by the strollers who worked the stagecoach circuits of the opening West. They were the staples of our Eastern theatres, which produced a succession of notable Shakespearean actors rivaling those of Great Britain. His audience and reading public were by no means an upper élite. On the Jersey cape where I spend my summers, old diaries record the meetings of a Shakespeare reading club in what was then a community of farmers and fishermen. In claiming its cultural heritage it was only being typical. Abraham Lincoln loved Shakespeare, as students of his prose might surmise, and once good-humoredly accepted a rebuke from the cultural establishment for daring to express a critical opinion.

Often the minor writers of a period supply the best clue to its affections because in them "influences" are less disguised. Turn for instance to one of the popular tales of the eighteen-forties, "Those Old Lunes; or, Which Was the Madman?"

by W. Gilmore Simms. It is about comical high jinks on the Mississippi border such as might now appear in a pulp "Western," but its title is followed by a quotation from *Hamlet* and its first two sentences each lift a phrase from that play. When the narrator proceeds to describe his twin sweethearts, "one or other of whom still usurped the place of a bright particular star in my most capacious fancy," the prose almost becomes blank verse. And observe: "still usurped" is Shakesperean for "always occupied"; "bright particular star" comes directly from *All's Well;* and "most capacious fancy" is a distillation of a speech on the sensibility of lovers by Orsino in *Twelfth Night.* There is so much Shakespeare that there is little Simms; the author is reveling in a language he and his readers loved. The style of "Those Old Lunes" we would not wish to revive; still, something of value may have passed out of currency with it. One fears that a blanket rejection of the "flowery" has made Shakespeare sound to many modern readers only like a more difficult Simms.

Of course the nineteenth-century rapport derived from something more than a fondness for rhythmic tropes. An age fully responds to a poet only when it responds to his values. He cannot thrive upon technical superiority, or intellectual challenge, or long-established prestige. He can only appear to do so. The genuine currency of any body of poetry depends on what may be called the currency of answering sentiments. Take for instance the lovely lines of Sonnet 96—

> Love's not Time's fool, though rosy lips and cheeks
> Within his bending sickle's compass come.

They could be truly experienced at a time when Tom Moore's "Believe me if all those enduring young charms" was enchanting the concert-going élite and "Silver threads among the gold" was being sung (with fervor) about the family harmonium. High and low could both understand and be moved, whereas now, those most capable of penetrating the highly figurative language are the ones least capable of responding to the sentiment expressed. The Darby and Joan icon no longer adorns any but the most humble interiors; among the cultivated, notice of a golden wedding anniversary is apt to evoke only mild wonder at human capacity for endurance. For half a century fear of sentimentality has been so pervasive that the gentler emotions appear to have atrophied, and literally thousands of Shakespeare's more delicate shafts rebound blunted from sedulously hardened hearts. There was actually a time when listeners *thrilled* to hear Orlando describe Rosalind's stature as "just as high as my heart." Imagine the answering apathy of audiences now, on Broadway or off!

A moment ago I spoke of Shakespeare's role in the imaginative life of the nineteenth century. The Cordelia image—that of a daughter still faithful and tender although despitefully used is ubiquitous in its fiction. It occurs so often in Dickens as to seem almost obsessive. We no longer encounter this image in fiction, and the reason is not far to seek. What Lear asks of his daughter, that she say she loves him, is nothing to what Shakespeare asks of her, that she *really* love him, deeply, selflessly, compassionately. Such filial devotion is so far out of fashion that it is viewed as none too wholesome. Can one truly experience *King Lear* if one must *try* to sympathize with its heroine, try *not* to sympathize with her wicked sisters, when everybody knows that an old man in the house is a nuisance, a demanding old man a pernicious nuisance? An equal effort is required of one confronted with the intense grief of Hamlet over the death of his father. Even Eliot was sufficiently a child of his times to find Hamlet's emotion "inexpressible because it is in excess of the facts as they appear." Probably no age before our own would find the o'erhasty marriage of one's mother to the murderer of one's father too trival a circumstance to be truly upsetting.

The Shakespearean conception of the binding nature of human attachments, within the family and without, is certain to meet resistance in a period of planned or unplanned obsolescence. What he presents as "natural" and even exemplary conduct is apt to be construed as psychopathic. Thus Hamlet's emotion becomes "expressible" (by commentators) if attributed to unconscious incestuous drives. When characters express the wish to die when their liege lords, friends, or masters die, as do Faulconbridge, Horatio, Kent, Eros, the properly conditioned modern observer suspects homosexuality. The fact that he is mistaken is not the point at issue. Dramatic poetry requires us to share a character's grief, not diagnose his ailments; we should be sympathetic, not suspicious. One fears, moreover, that these compelling personal attachments which so mislead the sophisticated can only confuse the naïve.

There are obstacles to understanding in the least recherché areas of conduct, especially where sex is concerned. Shakespeare habitually associates promiscuity with sickness, continence with virility, marital success with fecundity, and so on. The present tendency is to reverse such concepts. What he deferred to as appealing feminine reticence is now often identified as "frigidity." The nineteenth century was disturbed by his frankness, especially his ribald jokes, but as we examine his text now, we must wonder how any expurgator less morbidly sensitive than Bowdler could have found himself work to do. The pornographic explosion in current cinema, drama, and fiction is establishing norms of expectation which Shakespeare cannot meet on even approximately equal terms, and the questing reader must be left, like Antony in the absence of Cleopatra, gazing on vacancy.

Nowhere is Shakespeare's declining visibility better illustrated than in those theatrical productions where the director stages not the text but the "subtext"—meaning the play which Shakespeare would have written if he had possessed the director's genius. This usually means the transformation of the idyllic shearing feast into an orgy, the woodland sprite into a pimp, at least one character (chosen at random) into a pervert, the sage oldster into an idiot, the moral maxim into a yak line, and so on. A few of these exercises are socially well-intentioned, as when an aristocratic milieu is vulgarized in the interest of "democracy," or a war play is beaten into a peace play like a sword into a ploughshare, but they offer no evidence of the playwright's power of survival. Sometimes the novel effects derive less from pure invention than from a detail actually present in the text, seized upon and monstrously inflated as something audiences will *like*. There is little comfort in the fact that this meretricious Shakespeare is no more dreary than honest Shakespeare played without skill or conviction. If the plays must thus be made "relevant to our times," the productions are acts of salvage, and acts of salvage imply a prior catastrophe. We must face the possibility that the supposedly unsinkable Shakespeare has come to grief on twentieth-century shores, changed by our roiled seas into bones more strange than rich.

The idea that the stuffy Victorians may have been in a better position than ourselves to appreciate so well-certified a writer as Shakespeare is not an agreeable one. Neither is the idea that even the greatest works of literary art may share in some measure in the impermanence of the appeal of their content. Still, there the witnesses stand—not only the biographers whose "real" Shakespeare is Bacon, Oxford, or Marlowe, and the directors whose "real" Shakespeare is Beckett, Genet, or Grotowski, but also the critics whose "real" Shakespeare is Frazer, Sartre, or Freud. All seem to be busy stuffing out the empty garments of the deceased. Of course there is a chance that their efforts are misdirected. At the time of the Restoration a good deal of similarly ghoulish activity was in evidence, although Shakespeare had not departed but only passed out of the field of vision of certain literary and theatrical men of fashion. His works were twice reprinted unchanged while being treated as obsolete by the Tates and Rymers of the age. Perhaps the present situation shows points of resemblance. There are still persons who seem to find the plays relevant without outside assistance, who would rather read them than see them in mangled stage versions, and who shun disquisitions on what they *really* mean. It may be that fewer and fewer people uncontrolled by the fashionmakers in art are interested in art at all, but in our populous world even minorities run to considerable size. The stubborn remnant is represented even among college undergraduates. It is reassuring to see young eyes light up in response to an old sentiment—"Love's not Time's Fool." In the year 1909 Mark Twain, to whom the works of Shakespeare were scarcely distinguishable from those of Sir Walter Scott (and who was, coincidentally, a fanatic Baconian), promulgated the question "Is Shakespeare dead?" The answer "Yes" may still be premature.

5 EXTRICATING THE SONNETS

$\mathcal{S}$HORT of complete oblivion, the worst thing that can happen to a poem is for it to become controversial, since it then suffers the partial oblivion of becoming a part of something not itself. To retrieve Shakespeare's sonnets one should read one's own selection of the best, arranged in random order, never having heard, or trying to forget, anything ever said about them. Explanation of a kind often helpful to the reader of our older poetry will not be helpful here since it is bound to be, or to seem to be, tendentious. It cannot inform us about them because no certain information about them exists, except that all were written by someone before 1609 and two were written before 1599. The fact that Shakespeare was known in 1598 for "sugred Sonnets among his priuate friends" tells us nothing for certain about the date or authorship of any of the sonnets we have.

That all but the last two (as arranged in Thorpe's edition of 1609) are by Shakespeare is an opinion I share, but it is far from being a certainty. Thorpe was capable of fathering on Shakespeare, as had been done before, a miscellany of verses by divers hands. That he has not done so, except to the minor extent indicated by the presence of sonnets 153 and 154 (and the equally dubious *Lover's Complaint*), is a critical conclusion, objectively undemonstrable by any process thus far employed. We recognize the poetry of Shakespeare as we recognize the voice of an unseen acquaintance, and in particular instances we may be deceived. If the sonnet usually attributed to Drayton, "Since there's no help, come let us kiss and part," had slipped into Thorpe's edition, and was

Adapted from "Dating Shakespeare's Sonnets," *Shakespeare Quarterly,* vol. 1 (1950).

otherwise unknown, who would have challenged it? Or what amounts to the same thing, who could convince us that he would have challenged it?

I am not surrendering to skepticism, but trying to indicate that there can be no certainty in minor matters when there is no certainty in major ones, and a lust for it will bring only dusty answers. We must bring to the sonnets negative capability or miss them entirely. Anything said about them, being only a supposition, must be opposed by a countersupposition, until they are hemmed in to the point of invisibility. I shall explain further what I mean after I have added a few turrets to the wall of countersupposition about the date of the so-called "dating sonnets"—107, 123, and 124. The "consensus" opinion would place them, with the sequence in general, in the 1590's. Dr. Leslie Hotson would move them back, with the sequence in general, to the 1580's.[1] I would move them forward to the 1600's, but not the sequence in general, because I do not know what sonnets comprise what sequence.

None of the "dating sonnets" is dated by its general theme. Each treats of the permanence of love and immortalizing poetry, the transience of all things else. The theme was ancient and associated with a certain class of imagery. The couplet of 107—

> And thou in this shalte finde thy monument,
> When tyrants crests and tombs of brasse are spent.

need not be applied in Dr. Hotson's fashion to the crowns and tombs of King Philip and Pope Sixtus, who, incidentally, were frustrated but not entombed in 1588. Although the allusion to "pyramids" in Sonnet 123 does actually seem topical, as will be conceded in a moment, we must remember that poets writing in defiance of Time were prone to speak of the competitively defiant pyramids; they were, we might say,

---

[1] *Shakespeare's Sonnets Dated and Other Essays* (1949).

pyramid-suggestible. Bronze memorials, pyramids, and poetry had all been brought together by Horace:

> Exegi monumentum aere perennius
> regalique situ pyramidum altius . . .

The three sonnets in question, so far as their theme and external form are concerned, could have been written in any one of the twenty-five or thirty years preceding their publication. Their style—by which is meant here their music, and the concentration and integration of their language—suggests that they belong after rather than before the commonly assumed sonnet period, ca. 1593–ca. 1598. If compared with the sonnets incorporated in the early plays, with other lyrical passages in those plays, or with Shakespeare's narrative poems, it is hard to accept Dr. Hotson's argument that they were written by 1589. He has failed to give a complete picture of what the imagery of Sonnet 107 has suggested to scholars. If most of them have interpreted "mortall Moone" as applying to a living Elizabeth, it is because of their initial assumption that the sonnet was written before 1598. If shaken from this assumption they would not necessarily do so. In fact, a considerable number of scholars for a considerable period of time have dated Sonnet 107 in 1603, and their case has been strengthened in recent years by professors Mark Eccles and Garrett Mattingly.[2] I will illustrate the difficulty of eliminating the year 1603 as a possible date by giving samples of the type of symbolism most current in it. They have not been hard to find and could be multiplied ad nauseam.

Sonnet 107 reads:

> Not mine owne feares, nor the prophetick soule,
> Of the wide world, dreaming on things to come,

[2] G. Mattingly, "The Date of Shakespeare's Sonnet CVII," *PMLA*, vol. 48 (1933); M. Eccles, "The 'Mortal Moon' Sonnet," *TLS*, Feb. 15, 1934.

Can yet the lease of my true loue controule,
Supposde as forfeit to a confin'd doome.
The mortall Moone hath her eclipse indur'de,
And the sad Augurs mock their owne presage,
Incertenties now crowne them-selues assur'de,
And peace proclaimes Oliues of endlesse age.
Now with the drops of this most balmie time,
My loue lookes fresh, and death to me subscribes,
Since spight of him Ile liue in this poore rime,
While he insults ore dull and speachlesse tribes.
    And thou in this shalt finde thy monument,
    When tyrants crests and tombs of brasse are spent.

The early months of 1603 were among the blackest in English history: there was fear of Tyrone in Ireland, and of masterless men and malcontents at home; the Queen was dying and her successor unnamed; forty thousand Catholics were said to be ready to rise in arms if the successor should be James. "How could it be possible," said Thomas Dekker, "but that her sickness should throw abroad an vniuersall feare, and her death an astonishment?"[3] Then, as if by miracle, the crisis passed, and James ascended the English throne in an almost hysterical outburst of joy. That the astrological and historical background in 1603 was appropriate for the allusions of Sonnet 107 has been sufficiently argued by Eccles and Mattingly. Truly there were dire prognostications for 1588, as Hotson asserts, but Dekker informs us, "That same 88, which had more prophecies waiting at his heeles, than euer Merlin the Magitian had in his head, was a yeare of Iubile to this."[4] The mistaken "Augurs" of the sonnet appear also in verses by one J. Bowle:

[3] *The Wonderfull Yeare 1603,* in *Dekker's Non-Dramatic Works,* ed. A. B. Grosart, 5 vols. (London, 1884–1886), I, 87.
[4] Ibid., I, 87.

> Astrologers great wonder did assault,
> To find the cause; and yet were all deceiued.[5]

The chorus of lamentation for Elizabeth was followed by a chorus of panegyric for James—composed by Daniel, Drayton, Jonson, Dekker, Webster, and scores of lesser poets. If we can speak of such a thing as a season of a certain kind of imagery, this was the season of heavenly bodies, setting, rising, eclipsed, and so forth, and the season of "Oliues of endlesse age."

Dr. Hotson tells us interestingly that the Spanish armada was shaped like a crescent moon, but the moon had always been Elizabeth's symbol. She had been Cynthia herself, as in Lyly, or Cynthia's "imperial vot'ress" as in Shakespeare. In the elegiac chorus of 1603, she is Luna, Delia, Cynthia, Phoebe, Belphoebe (all the moon) when she is not the setting sun. Whether she could be described as a "mortall Moone" or as having endured an "eclipse" need not be debated theoretically. She *was* so described. In *Elizabetha quasi vivens,* Henry Petowe writes,

> Luna's extinct, and now behold the sunne
> Whose beames soake up the moysture of all tears.
> A phoenix from her ashes doth arise.... [6]

In a single volume, issued by the "Cambridge Muses" in 1603, the image recurs constantly.[7] Henry Campion writes,

> *For Phoebe gone, a Phoebus now doth shine,*
> Mars and Minerua's champion lets him call,
> England's strong shield, vnder whose sacred shine
> England may shake, but neare is like to fall.
> *Shine Phoebus stil, neare may thy vertuous lights*
> *Eclipsed be with black obscured nights.*

---

[5] *Sorrowes Ioy,* 1603, in *Progresses James I,* ed. J. Nichols, 4 vols. (London, 1828), I, 16.

[6] *Harleian Miscellany,* 10 vols. (1808–1813), X, 337.

[7] *Sorrowes Ioy,* 1603, pp. 12, 20, 23, 24 (italics mine).

From Edward Kellet we get,

> Take comfort, heauie minde,
> For *though thy moone decaies, thy sun doth rise;*
> Which (but shee, had any shin'd)
> Would, past all admiration, rule our skies,
> And now will farre surpasse
> The most large vnbound hopes we could expect . . .

Thomas Walkington's version of the metaphor casts James as *Cynthius:*

> *Faire Cynthia's dead: so is my Muse,* she breathes;
> My muse it breathes; yet cannot speake for griefe.
> She's dead, her death no life my Muse bequeathes,
> *Sole Cynthius yeelds my dying muse releefe,*
> Twixt both my liue-dead Muse as yron lies
> Between two adamants of equall prize.

In the contribution of E.L., Elizabeth becomes the sun, but, observe, a sun *eclipst:*

> As late when Winter had cast off his weede
> *Our sunne eclipst did set, oh, light most faire,*
> Calme was the time, tempests and stormes agreed
> To hide their heads, and not disturbe the aire.
> *Next morne, fair Phoebe, betime mounts on his steed,*
> And to the azurd heauens makes repaire. . . .

Actually "mortall Moone" could have been applied to a living Elizabeth, without those sinister connotations with which Dr. Hotson invests the word "mortall." King James in 1603 was called a *"mortal God."*[8] The term "mortall Moone" aptly describes the Armada, but the continuation of the line "hath her eclipse indur'de" seems too gentle to express a mood of exultation over a great victory. The Armada had been de-

---

[8] John Savile, *Salutatorie Poem,* in *Progresses James I,* ed. J. Nichols, I, 140.

stroyed. Elizabeth, in English sentiment of 1603, had endured an eclipse. In the words "our Terrene Moone is now Eclipst," quoted by Dr. Hotson, Mark Antony is describing a defeat not a victory.

In the numerous, and almost endless, panegyrics of James, Peace and Plenty, with olives as the symbol of both, provided the dominant theme. Richard Martin, welcoming the King on behalf of the Sheriffs of London at Stamford Hill in 1603, said "The people shall every one sit under his own olive tree, and anoynt himself with the fat thereof . . ."[9] For Thomas Dekker the olive tree had replaced the cedar: "The Cedar of her gouvernment which stood alone and bare no fruie, is changed now to an oliue, vpon whose spreading branches grow both Kings and Queenes."[10] The symbolism of the olive tree was used visually as well as verbally. Ben Jonson in describing the pageant at Temple Bar during the King's welcome into London, says, "The first and principall person in the temple, was IRENE, or Peace, shee was placed aloft in a Cant; her attyre white, semined with starres, her haire loose and large: a wreathe of oliue on her head, on her shoulder a siluer doue: in her left hand, shee held forth an oliue branch, with a handfull of ripe eares, in the other a crowne of laurell, as notes of victorie and plentie."[11] It is little wonder that Gervase Markham wrote retrospectively that King James entered England not simply with an olive branch in his hand "but with a whole Forrest of Olives round about him . . ."[12]

The Horatian tradition behind the concluding couplet of

---

[9] *A Speach,* in *Progresses James I,* ed, J. Nichols, I, 130.

[10] *The Wonderfull Yeare 1603,* p. 97.

[11] *Ben Jonson His Part of King James his Royall and Magnificent Entertainment,* 1604, in *Ben Jonson,* ed. C. H. Herford and P. Simpson, 11 vols. (Oxford, 1925–1952), VII, 106.

[12] *Honour in his Perfection,* 1625, quoted by Mattingly, "Date of Sonnet CVII," p. 721.

Sonnet 107 has been mentioned above, but the question might arise of whether *tyrants tombs* would be mentioned, even privately, by an English writer in a poem associated with the death of Elizabeth. There is no real difficulty here. In the presence of Death, Elizabeth qualified *poetically* as a tyrant. One of the most eulogistic published epitaphs contains the lines,

> Loe, here for signe, how Death hath equall made
> The Princely scepter and the deluers spade.[13]

James Shirley seems to have remembered these lines in 1658 when he wrote,

> Sceptre and Crown
> Must tumble down
> And in the dust be equal made
> With the poor crooked scythe and spade.[14]

If we were to give Shirley's famous dirge any application other than to the fatal contest of Ajax and Ulysses which seems to evoke it, it would probably be to the death of Cromwell because Shirley was a royalist. But poets have a faculty for confusing party lines. We are reminded of the dirge in *Cymbeline*—

> Fear no more, the frown o' th' great;
> Thou are past the tyrant's stroke.

But the reigning king is Cymbeline, no tyrant at all but only a temporarily misguided father.

The topical portion of Sonnet 123 reads as follows:

> No! Time, thou shalt not bost that I doe change,
> Thy pyramyds buylt vp with newer might
> To me are nothing nouell, nothing strange,

---

[13] Excerpted by J. Nichols, *Progresses Elizabeth,* 3 vols. (1788), III, 651.
[14] *Contention of Ajax and Ulysses,* 1658.

> They are but dressings of a former sight:
> Our dates are breefe, and therefor we admire,
> What thou dost foyst vpon vs that is ould,
> And rather make them borne to our desire,
> Then thinke that we before haue heard them tould:
> Thy registers and thee I both defie ...

Dr. Hotson takes the "pyramyds buylt vp with newer might" to be the Egyptian obelisks set up in Rome by Pope Sixtus between 1586 and 1589. But if we consider the sonnet as being written in 1603, we need not go abroad. As part of their welcome to King James, the companies of London and the foreign merchants commissioned hundreds of joiners and other craftsmen to erect imposing structures at various stations about the city and Westminster. Most of these were temple facades or triumphal arches, but they incorporated *pyramids*, and, in the opinion of Dekker at least, they put the obelisks of Sixtus in the shade:

> The Mausolæan tombe,
> The sixteene curious gates in Rome,
>   Which times preferre,
> Both past and present, Neroe's Theatre,
>   That in one day was all gilt ore,
>   Add to these more,
> Those columnes and those pyramids that won
> Wonder by height, the Colosse of the Sun;
> *Th' Aegyptian Obelisks are all forgotten,*
> *Onely their names grow great, themselves be rotten.*[15]

Although the highest of the structures was no more than ninety feet, in the contemporary imagination "these wonders of wood clymde ... into the clouds." The structure at the Royal Exchange included four hollow pyramids lighted from

[15] Stephen Harrison, *The Arches of Triumph*, 1603 (text without plates printed by Nichols, *Progresses James I*, I, 332), italics mine.

within: "So they did shine afarre off like Crysolites, and sparkled like Carbuncles." The structure at the Entrance to Cheapside consisted of "Pedestalles, Balles, and Pyramides, devowring in their full vpright heigh, from the ground line to the top, just 60. foote."[16] Stephen Harrison's engravings show the structure at Soper Lane to have had the most conspicuous pyramidal motif. Its two richly ornamented "pyramids" may be described as engaged obelisks and are quite impressive. No engraving survives for the "device" erected in the Strand, but it is thus described by Ben Jonson: "The inuention was a Raine-bow, the Moone, Sunne, and those Seuen Starres, which antiquitie hath styl'd the Pleides, or Vergiliae, aduanced betweene two magnificent Pyramids, of 70 feet in height, on which were drawne his Majesties seuerall pedigrees, Eng. and Scot."[17] That there was available for allusion in Shakespeare's immediate world of 1603–04 something "novel" and "strange," pyramids built up with "newer might" from old models and therefore "but dressings of a formcr sight," would seem indisputable.

I have nothing to add in the way of materials for interpreting the imagery in Sonnet 124. Nearly any year in Tudor and Stuart history offers events that would render the allusions in the first twelve lines topical in a sense, and the concluding couplet, although perhaps less widely applicable, seems to me invulnerably ambiguous. If indeed the

foles of time,
Which die for goodnes, who haue liu'd for crime

were men who died martyrs in their own eyes but not the poet's, the lines could have been written at any time during

---

[16] Thomas Dekker, *The Magnificent Entertainment,* 1604, in *Dramatic Works of Thomas Dekker,* ed. F. Bowers, 4 vols. (Cambridge, 1953–1961), II, 370, 375.

[17] Ben Jonson, *His Part . . . ,* p. 106.

the Jesuit mission. Disregarding, then, the "dating" significance of Sonnet 124, and admitting at least the possibility that
Sonnets 107 and 123 were written in 1603–04, observe the
nature of the fallout.

Our minds veer at once to the biographical interpretations
of the sonnets, with the accompanying attempts to identify
that ubiquitous trio, fair youth, dark lady, rival poet. Just as
1593–1598 is the favored period of composition, so is the Earl
of Southampton the favored candidate as fair youth. But his
age has proved an inconvenience since even in 1593 he was
twenty, only nine years younger than the poet, who describes
himself as beaten and chopped with "tanned antiquity." If
Sonnet 107 was written in 1603, Southampton was thirty, the
father of a growing family, the veteran of several military
campaigns abroad and an abortive rebellion at home, and just
removed from the shadow of the executioner's axe. Could he
be the "sweet boy" of the sonnet immediately following? and
the "lovely boy" of Sonnet 126?

The replies will vary. Someone may say that his candidate
has never been Lord Southampton anyway, but Lord Pembroke, who was of appropriately tender years in 1593 and only
twenty-three in 1603. Dr. Hotson will point out that his candidate is no hereditary lord at all, but William Hatcliffe, the
young "Prince of Purpoole" of the Gray's Inn revels of 1588–
89 in which year *he* dates the sonnet. Obviously all we have
done is set in motion another parade of the phantoms to inter-
cept our view. None of the sonnets specify that the fair youth
is a lord, actual or honorary, or of any higher social rank than
the poet, even though more fortunately situated in life. In
view of Elizabethan usage, the "friend" in some of the sonnets
could be a younger brother or imaginary son. A person wish-
ing to defend the candidacy of Southampton may say that
Sonnet 107 itself does not mention the youth of the friend,
and might apply to that somewhat weatherbeaten lord even

in 1603. Sonnets 108 and 126 addressing him as a "boy" are simply out of order; they should have been printed earlier in the sequence.

But if the sonnets are not in proper order in the received text, there is no "sequence." If we are permitted to arrange our own choice of sonnets in our own order, we can make them tell a variety of stories with a changing dramatis personae. Over a hundred of the sonnets, more than two-thirds of all, fail to specify the sex of the supposed recipient, and are linked only by association (Thorpe's) with the story of fair youth, dark lady, and rival poet. Out of these it would be easy to construct a "sequence" celebrating William's courtship and happy marriage, concluding with sonnet 116 addressed to Anne on the occasion of their twenty-fifth wedding anniversary.

A remark like the last will not clarify the air. Rather it will increase the density of the fallout to the point of asphyxiation, because it sounds like a shot in the campaign to represent the sonnets as "wholesome." The identity of the fair youth has been less diversionary than speculations about the poet's relations with him. In certain sonnets scattered through the collection, but concentrated chiefly toward its end, a situation does actually emerge. That the poet's love for the youth is pure, as distinct from his lust for a certain loose matron, is the *donnée* of this situation. The whole point is that a friendship is blighted by the intrusion of a sensuality external to it, and the poet is afflicted by the faithlessness of his mistress, who proves that his friend is as corruptible as himself. Since Thorpe's collection was issued simply as *Shake-speares Sonnets,* it was naturally viewed as autobiographical, and early commentators were chiefly troubled by the poet's role as self-confessed (though penitent) adulterer. Their situation was enviable.

A more acute sense of discomfort was felt as time passed

and the rules governing the language of friendship became increasingly restrictive. No proper man would say that he "loved" another man or would praise his "beauty." Shakespeare had not only done so repeatedly and with fervor, but had violated many other nineteenth-century principles of manly decorum of expression. The assumption that all of the sonnets not specifically addressed to the mistress were addressed to the fair youth added to the discomfort by building the supply of troubling suggestion to massive proportions. That there was a hint here of what the Elizabethans called, in their least emphatic term, a "strange love" was obviously feared, and the issue was at last brought into the open by Oscar Wilde and others who had a personal interest in establishing its presence. They found confirmation in the exciting knowledge that on Shakespeare's stage the parts of women were performed by boys.

The consequence is that it is now impossible to say anything right about the emotional content of the sonnets. Homosexuals are inclined to share Wilde's view, and it would be inhumane to deny them its comfort, but since our humane impulses should be inclusive, we must recognize that endorsing the view will not contribute to the greatest comfort of the greatest number. Attacking the view is an equally dubious tactic. Needless defenses of Shakespeare's heterosexuality can only advertise that it has been questioned, while a notably vigorous defense might seem intended to advertise the speaker's own sexual normality. Even silence on the subject can be damaging if one is mentioning the sonnets at all, because it will seem to signal fear of probing a tender area.

The relaxed, tolerant, eclectic attitude so characteristic of the present day proves not the ideal answer either, because, oddly enough, it has produced more distracting absurdities of explanation than others. It has actually been argued in print that whereas Shakespeare himself was "straight," the fair youth and rival poet were not. The route to this conclusion is too devious for me to follow. More common is the position that the poet was unaware of his own propensities, and unconsciously exposed them in his sonnets. The proof is that these show that he was capable of loving another man. But surely we would know this to be the case even if he had never written a sonnet. The capability is revealed in the plays, in which no epicene taint has been traced, and the sonnets openly proclaim it. Of what propensities was he unconscious? If a man's faith in his own heterosexuality is based on his incapability of loving another man, is he not somewhat maimed? I shall not pursue ramifications—for instance the peculiar idea that the very frankness with which he discloses his love of the youth is a kind of Proustian disguise in reverse. This way madness lies.

It was the opinion of Alexander Dyce and some equally responsible scholars of his day that the biographical significance of the sonnets is minimal, that they are in the main imaginative exercises in verse. To what extent this opinion was formed in retreat from the idea of Shakespeare as adulterer, or worse, must remain conjectural, but it has less utility than might appear. Up to a point it must be accepted as valid. For instance, in fifteen sonnets clustered at the beginning of Thorpe's edition, Shakespeare says precisely the same thing in fifteen different ways: that a certain person, usually specified as a young man, should perpetuate his beauty by marrying and having a child, usually specified as a son. The mind boggles at the idea that these sonnets were written with a practical end in view. One or two of them yes, but not fifteen; a youth so bombarded might be driven to vows of eternal celibacy. It is not from this group alone that one receives the impression that the poet is simply exercising himself. Often changes are rung upon identical sentiments or ideas. My obligations as editor once required me to gloss the entire series, and I found to my surprise that I was sometimes repelled by the poet's unflagging ingenuity. All of the sonnets bear witness to their having been written by a great poet, but only a minority of them are great poems. Must we think of the latter simply as the most successful of certain experiments in versifying? Perhaps we would prefer to trace them to censurable emotions rather than to none at all.

Specters withdraw and miasmal mists clear away if we remind ourselves of certain facts. The "dating sonnets" are so few and their evidence so equivocal that the truth finally borne in upon us is that we are dealing here with the least topical poetry in the world. And whatever the meaning of the arrangement of the sonnets, Thorpe's or another's, every arrangement is composed of individual sonnets, some of which are great. Not one of the latter can be dated (in any sense of the term). Not one is intrinsically related to the story of fair youth, dark lady, rival poet. Not one is intrinsically suggestive of any state of abnormal psychology. Not one gains anything in meaning or effect by being read in conjunction with any other sonnet. And of course not one reads like a mere exercise in writing verse. In the case of these great poems all talk about the identity of the recipient, however sensible or silly, and all psychological diagnoses, biographical speculations, and moral charges or vindications are equally intrusive and irrelevant. Since I seem, paradoxically, to be loudly clamoring for silence, I must add a word of self-defense. A few of Shakespeare's sonnets have long had the power to move me more deeply than any other passages in English poetry. Naturally I believe that in these sonnets which unlock my heart Shakespeare was unlocking his, but I have never told anyone what he should take them to mean or even which ones they are.

6 COSMIC CARD GAME

*T*HE VULGAR error that Shakespeare's *Antony and Cleopatra* is a tragedy about Antony and Cleopatra has been perpetuated by so-called learned men. An appallingly self-exposive note "elucidates" the text in the edition by the late Professor Kittredge:

> ... she, Eros, has
> Pack'd cards with Caesar and false-play'd my glory
> Unto an enemy's triumph. (IV. xiv.18–20)

"Triumph," explains Kittredge with pathetic eagerness, meant not only a victory-celebration but also "a trump card." It is not that the note is *wrong*. In its feeble way, it is, of course, *right*. What so distresses the quickened sensibilities of our time is that only after he had reached the fourth act of a work established by Mr. Eliot as Shakespeare's greatest was the commentator able to perceive, and then but dimly, one isolated detail of a pattern of imagery that articulates the entire drama and gives it form and meaning. He fails wholly to observe that the richly ambivalent word "triumph" was also the name of *the Elizabethan card game from which modern whist and contract bridge have descended.*

There are in *Antony and Cleopatra* five laminated patterns of iterative imagery: the Chaos Pattern, the Bedclothes Pattern, the Insect Pattern, the Alcoholic Beverage Pattern, and the Card Game Pattern. The last carries the theme and obtrudes upon the consciousness of the properly qualified reader the shifting partnerships, the play and false-play, the, so to speak, *brouillamini à jouer* in a Cosmic Game of Triumph.

Reprinted from the *American Scholar*, vol. 20 (1951).

The first piece in the pattern is inserted in the first speech of the play:

> PHILO: His Captain's *heart,*
> Which in the scuffles of great fights hath burst
> The buckles on his breast, *reneges* all temper. (1.i.6–8)

The word "reneges" (occurring here and here only in Shakespeare) establishes Antony as a negligent, not dishonest, gamester, and juxtaposed with "great fights" sets up at once a paradoxical equation of the trivial with the momentous. Much of the effect of the Card Game imagery lies in the ironical excess or over-adequacy of the action of the drama as an objective correlative for the thematic pattern of language.

The word "heart" is the first of two hundred and forty-seven instances (one instance I have eliminated as doubtful) in which the iconographic element in the pattern occurs. Each of the four rulers in the play is made to resemble an honor card in one of the four suits. Cleopatra is the Queen of Clubs (self-described as the trefoil or "full-blown rose . . . with Phoebus' amorous pinces black," 1.v. 28). Lepidus is the King of Diamonds (utilizing as pun the Latin, *lapides,* gems, in color red, "Lepidus is high colour'd," 11.vii.5). Octavius Caesar is the Knave of Spades ("he's but Fortune's knave," v.ii.3; in color black, "has a cloud in's face," 111.ii.52). Antony is the King of Hearts, as will so abundantly appear as to need no present illustration. If my reader will glance at the King of Hearts and Knave of Spades in his modern deck, the design of which was standardized in Tudor times, he will note the marvelous consistency in the drama of allusions to "Antonius's beard" (11.ii.7) and "the scarce-bearded Caesar" (1.i.21). Lesser honor cards are Alexas (Cleopatra's "foul knave," 1.ii.75), Eros (Antony's "dear knave," iv.xiv.14), and Thyreus ("This Jack of Caesar's," 111.xiii.103). Through her unhappy state-marriage with Antony, Octavia of course figures as the

Queen of Hearts. (That Shakespeare has injected into his poem, through this detail, a touch of human sentiment, the critic must concede even though he may not wholly approve.)

In what follows, two points must be kept in mind: first, that in the imagistic play at cards, over which the cruder action of the drama lies as on palimpsest, no higher card than a King is mentioned—the ACE *never;* and second, that although Antony, Cleopatra, Caesar, and the rest are playing cards, they also the cards *played*. The profound significance of the twin paradox, providing no less than the clue to the total meaning of the drama, will be treated in conclusion.

Although co-rulers of the Roman Empire, the words "competitor" and "partner" are used interchangeably wherever Antony and Caesar are concerned (i.iv.3; ii.ii.22; ii.vii.76; v.i.42 inter alia). In the first rubber, the competitor-partners have won a bid in hearts, owing largely to Caesar's ability to strengthen that suit by offering his sister Octavia to Antony. Caesar is dummy while Antony plays the hand:

> ANTONY: Let me have your *hand*.
> Further this act of grace; and from this hour
> The *heart* of brothers govern in our loves
> And sway our great designs.
>   CAESAR: There is my *hand*.
> A *sister* I bequeath you, whom no brother
> Did ever love so dearly. Let her live
> To join our kingdoms and our *hearts*. (ii.ii.148-54)

Graphically evoked is the picture of the two facing each other across the table, the cards in play before them. Antony leads the Queen of Hearts, and an onlooker later describes the tense moment to Cleopatra:

> MESSENGER: I looked her in the *face,* and saw her *led*
> Between her brother and Mark Antony. (iii.iii.12-13)

Backed by Antony's own King, the card is high and should establish the suit ("settle the *heart* of Antony," II.ii.246), but Caesar thinks it should have been reserved, "cherished," whereupon bickering begins between the competitor-partners. The card itself, termed by Caesar "poor castaway," thus plaintively laments:

> Ay me most wretched
> That have my *heart* parted betwixt two friends
> That do afflict each other. (III.vi.76–78)

Now distrusting Antony's card-sense, the prudent Caesar covers his stake by wagering against his own side, as has been his custom:

> Caesar gets money
> Where he loses hearts. (II.i.13–14)

Antony, resenting what seems to him alienated loyalty, charges his partner with laying reluctantly in the dummy hand such honor-cards as he may possess:

> when perforce he could not
> But pay me terms of *honour,* cold and sickly
> He *vented* them. (III.iv.6–8)

The post-mortem in act III, scene vi, features Antony's querulous claim to a share in Caesar's winnings, and the dissolution of their partnership.

We must pause here to note the rare distinction in Shakespeare's artistry. Although we need not stain our page with the so-called historical approach to literature, or proceed to Shakespeare through the purlieus of the minor dramatists, brief mention may be made of Thomas Heywood. Those who have read *A Woman Killed with Kindness* with the attentiveness evoked by Mr. Eliot's devastating analysis will recall the metaphoric use of card game terms in the banal and sentimental course of act III. The imagery in *Antony and Cleopatra,* while, of course, never so unspeakably jejune, is sometimes equally perspicuous, its superiority lying less in a guarded transparency than in a consistent sustenation—the true measure, after all, of the distance between Shakespeare and Heywood. Now observe how the master employs gaming imagery to forewarn us that even so seasoned a player as Antony will prove no match for Caesar. Antony says,

> Be it art or hap
> . . . the very dice obey him. (II.iii.33)

"Dice" being the plural of "die," and "die" signifying the climax of sexual experience as every schoolboy knows, at least in the better private institutions, "The very dice [climaxes] obey him" signifies that Caesar has his passions under almost repellently complete control. (Although it seems improbable that the number should be greater or less than seven, the present author has deliberated over whether the "dice" image may not offer an *eighth* type of ambiguity; prudently he shrinks back from making the suggestion until he may take counsel with his correspondents, one of whom is, unfortunately, en route to the Lower Punjab.)

In act III the inevitable occurs, and Antony resumes his former partnership with Cleopatra, that avid gamester ("pour out the pack," II.v.54) who since the opening of the drama has been lamenting her forced abstention from play. Antony begins the game in an exhilarated mood:

> My *playfellow,* your *hand,* this kingly seal
> And *plighter of high hearts!* (III.xiii.125–26)

Observe that Antony insists upon frequent bids in hearts, although Cleopatra is permitted to play most of the hands. As the play proceeds, we become increasingly aware of Caesar at this table also, but now in the avowed role of formidable opponent. Antony grows irritated, complaining at the run of cards:

> Of late, when I cried 'Ho!'
> Like boys unto a muss, *kings* would start forth ...
> Take hence this *Jack* ... (III.xiii.90–93)

He sneers at Caesar's skill, suggesting that his servant Thyreus is as capable as his master, being "one that ties his points" (III.xiii.156). Dexterously developed is the imagistic foreshadowing of that climactic misplay when Cleopatra will lead her King (Antony) into Caesar's trump. Antony's words are a warning to his partner:

> If I lose my *honour*,
> I lose *myself*. (III.iv.22–23)

But the play is made, as signaled in the wry words of Canidius, "So our leader's *led*/And we are women's *men* (III.vii.70–71)." We get Antony's anguished outcry, "O, whither hast thou *led* me, Egypt?" (III.xi.51), and his incredulous examination of the lost trick, "Where hast thou been, my *heart?*" (III.xiii.173). It was at this stage that Kittredge caught his one fleeting glimpse of Shakespeare's intention, and composed his little note on Antony's accusation that Cleopatra has "pack'd cards" with Caesar and "false-play'd" his glory "unto an enemy's triumph."

Without displaying that literal-mindedness so delectably satirized in *How Many Children Had Lady Macbeth?* by Mr. L. C. Knights, one of the distinguished *Scrutiny* wits, we may perhaps ask whether Cleopatra actually *did* pack cards with Caesar, and whether Dolabella's description of Antony ("he is pluck'd," III.xii.4) is to be taken at face value. That Cleopatra is a cheat goes without saying, and there is ample indication that there has been cheating in the present rubber. (Before it is over there are six Kings in the deck: "Six kings already/Show me the way to yielding," III.x.33). Quite early we have heard of Antony "being barber'd ten times o'er" (II.ii.229), and it is quite possible that taking him to the barber has become habitual with her, but *it does not follow* that her cheating is designed to aid Caesar. Her lead in hearts seems to have been a genuine error, no doubt induced by confusion during her covert manipulation of the cards, and Antony himself finally adopts this view. He proceeds with the game, although with the poorest of hands, consisting, on the action level of the drama, only of servitors and old captains. These must be thought of as spot cards in the suit of hearts ("fiery spots," I.iv.12), and, as Enobarbus warns, capable of taking only "odd tricks." Antony, nevertheless, speaks with bravado:

> Know, my *hearts,*
> I hope well of tomorrow and will *lead* you. (IV.iii.41–42)

A speech by Scarus, no doubt enigmatical to those who read on the plot level alone, becomes richly meaningful in the light of the Card Game Pattern:

> I had a wound here that was like a T,
> But now 'tis made an H. (IV.vii.7–8)

That is to say, the *hearts* ("H"), however low, are at the moment *trumps* ("T"). Antony wins his few "odd tricks" and Scarus eagerly takes them in:

> Let us score their *backs*
> And snatch 'em up. (IV.vii.12–13)

It will be remembered that the surface action of the drama in act IV, scenes v, vi, vii, and viii, is entirely concerned with Antony's successful but hopelessly futile sortie against Caesar's encompassing army. The way in which the irony of this success-failure is underlined by the mood music of trumpets is one of the most subtly amazing effects of the *Triumph*

Imagery. The stage directions order trumpets to sound in all these scenes, and, in the last, Antony orders, "Trumpeter,/ With brazen din blast you the city's ears" (IV.viii.35-36). Now bearing in mind that, as even Kittredge perceived, "triumph" signifies "trump," it follows that "trump" signifies "triumph." Therefore "trumpets" (or "trump-ettes") signifies "triumph-ettes"—or *hollow victories*.

After Antony's "self hand" has taken his own life, has "triumph'd [trumped] on itself" (IV.xv.15), he may be considered as permanently retired from play. For a brief interval, Cleopatra contemplates playing alone, but for a person of her temperament there is no stimulus in Solitaire: "patience is sottish" (IV.xv.79). Her faith in a better run of cards is soon restored—"my hands I'll trust," (IV.iv.49)—and the fifth act finds her trying to match skill with Caesar. Eagerly she demands the deal—"Quick, quick, good hands!" (v.ii.39). The play in act v, scene ii, is quick and decisive. The stake, consisting of Cleopatra and her treasure, is won by Caesar through his finesse with Dolabella. "For the Queen, I'll take her," says the latter. A moment later we hear her dazedly ask, "Is't not your trick?" and the reply, "Your loss is, as yourself, great." Then comes Cleopatra's hopeless, "He'll lead me then in triumph?" (v.ii.66,101,109), and the reply can be only Yes. She is now the trump card of Caesar, and the imagistic prophecy of act II, scene ii, line 189, where she is called "a most triumphant lady," is thus ironically fulfilled.

The manner in which our Queen of Clubs, by self-destruction, robs the winner of his triumph must be prefaced by a word of explanation. Throughout the drama, the lesser characters have themselves been busy at cards—their game not Triumph but one of a humbler sort. In act I, scene ii (rich in gaming imagery throughout), Charmian says, "Let me be married to three *kings* ... and companion me with my mistress." Since her mistress is a Queen, and only Queens can "companion" with Queens, it is obvious that Charmian is praying for a full-house-Kings-high. Now nothing is more striking in *Antony and Cleopatra* than the spectacle of deterioration in its titular characters, and the way the imagery suggests progressive vulgarity, as when Antony invites Cleopatra to sit on his lap and play his trump cards ("ride on the pants triumphing," iv.iii.16). As acts iv and v continue, the royal characters advert periodically to the more squalid game of their retainers, and we are thus prepared for the ruse by which Cleopatra saves herself from being led in trump by Caesar. The fatal asps are brought her by a *Clown,* and this *Clown,* far from being a tasteless intrusion upon the tragic close of the drama, is the crowning piece in the Pattern of Card Game Imagery. Into the game of Triumph is introduced, to Caesar's complete surprise, a type of card normally used only in the humble game of more lowly people—in a word, the Joker.

It is from the humbler game that the valedictory imagery of *Antony and Cleopatra* is drawn. The lovers had been called in the opening scene of the drama "a mutual pair" and, in the concluding speech, we hear,

> No grave upon the earth shall clip in it
> A *pair* so famous. (v.ii.362–63)

The objection that a *pair* consists, not of a King and Queen, but of two Kings or two Queens, has been deftly met by the poet as early as act i, scene iv, lines 5–7, with Caesar's statement that Antony

> . . . is not more manlike
> Than Cleopatra, nor the queen of Ptolemy
> More womanly than he,

thus effecting that sexual homogeneity necessary to "a mutual pair." To the objection sometimes plaintively made that the reader's mind is unable to retain the relationship between two such widely separated pieces of data in an imagistic pattern, we can only reply, if reply we must, that there is considerable difference in the strength of human *minds,* and that if we must ignore Shakespeare's intention merely because of the incapacity of the "generality," we might as well exclaim at once, with Amy Lowell, "God, what are patterns for!"

And thus we leave them, a *famous pair,* but *clipped* even in their grave—enclosed, that is, in the mendacious atmosphere of a gambling dive or clip joint. *It is a bitter play!*

Before putting into words my concluding revelation of the nature of *Antony and Cleopatra,* I must remark that the serious critic who would discharge with awareness his high office, and nurture such areas of sensibility as our era affords, must, sooner or later, as the greatest living critical, poetical, and spiritual guide himself unerringly perceived, consider Shakespeare. It is a taxing ministry, because Shakespearean drama has been so "clapper-clawed with the palms of the vulgar"—the indiscriminate and undiscriminating hordes of mere readers and playgoers—that the mere task of de-degradation seems simply overwhelming. The only way in which we can combat the distressing pervasiveness of poetic non-perceptivity is by patient effort. The present admittedly incomplete survey of the imagery of *Antony and Cleopatra* must illustrate to those who have viewed the work as a mere chronicle of love and empire that what Shakespeare has actually done has been to show in conflict the rational Caesar and the passionate Antony, with Cleopatra—a person of by no means unquestionable integrity—as a distinct factor in the latter's downfall. On the cosmic level, the new insights provided by adequate attention to the thematic imagery are even richer and more novel. The fact that the ACE is never played and *never can be played* by wordly actors, the fact that the characters are both players at cards and *cards played* intimates to us that Man's Destiny Is Not Wholly In His OWN HANDS. Once we have grasped the thought, we are amazed that it has not been grasped before, either in connection with this great drama or with an even greater object of contemplation—human life in general. Now that the idea dawns upon us, we realize that it has struggled for expression elsewhere in Shakespeare, notably in the Wood-Working-Imagery in *Hamlet:*

> There's a divinity that shapes our ends,
> Rough-hew them how we will.

The message, and I use the word unashamedly, brought to us by Shakespeare is, then, in last analysis, the message brought us by Mr. Eliot—the lesson of humility. It is with humility that I proffer it to the world.

*I*T SEEMS scarcely mannerly at this late date to discuss the historical importance of Kyd's *Spanish Tragedy*. The play has long been credited with introducing to the English popular stage the revenge motif, with its Senecan panoply of ghosts, multiple murders, dire auguries, moral sententiousness, and the like. With so many resemblances in fable, dramatis personae, and theatrical devices to Shakespeare's *Hamlet*, it must surely be considered portentous enough. Why encumber it further with the dubious honor of anticipating the methods of better plays?

Nevertheless, perhaps something remains to be said. It may be argued that our attention has been diverted by the conspicuous—that in observing the priority of Kyd's play within a specific genre we have somehow missed a point. I should like to propose that the historical importance of *The Spanish Tragedy* resides chiefly in certain details of its action. These may not properly be considered Senecan at all, and their influence is manifest not in the revenge plays alone but in nearly all subsequent popular tragedies except the documentary histories. I refer to the element of intrigue in Kyd's play, those considerable portions of it where the entertaining complication of the action becomes an end in itself. Perhaps Kyd's greatest innovation was to employ comic methods with tragic materials, thus creating a species of comitragedy. Maneuvers traditionally associated with the petty ends of petty tricksters are given a sensationally lethal turn so as to win a new and oddly mixed response—of amusement and horror, revulsion and admiration. To what extent such a response is destructive

From *Essays on Shakespeare and Elizabethan Drama in Honor of Hardin Craig,* ed. R. Hosley (Columbia, University of Missouri Press, 1962).

of the dignity of tragedy and its presumed spiritual ends is an open critical question.

Classical and earlier Renaissance tragedy contains, to be sure, elements of intrigue. An instance is offered by Seneca's *Thyestes*. The victim is lured to his destruction by a ruse, and grim elements of humor appear: Atreus is clever and Thyestes is a gull. But in a sense the Agamemnon of Aeschylus is also a gull, as are many tragic heroes, and a distinction must be made at once. When the emphasis is upon the facts as they are and the facts as they appear to the victim, the effort is tragic irony. When the emphasis is upon the means by which that difference is achieved, the effect is something else. The appeal of intrigue is intellectual. Moral judgment stands partly in abeyance as we check the villain's calculations. Whereas we watch Macbeth commit a murder, we watch Iago play a game. Classical tragedy, mainly retrospective in its method and traditional in its matter, could not elaborate the action very far. Elaboration to the point of anything we may properly call intrigue is possible only when invention is permissible, and the heart of the fable is presented in a series of progressive episodes. The fables treated in classical and neoclassical tragedies sometimes contained intrigue, but in the process of dramatization it was canceled by the structure, surviving as a mere potential. The New Comedy, as represented by Plautus and Terence, despite the concentration of the action, was preeminently drama of intrigue.

The distinction is obvious enough in practice. When Kyd's Lorenzo maneuvers Pedringano into slaying Serberine, the authorities into arresting Pedringano, and the latter into remaining silent until the moment of his execution because of the hope of a pardon, he is behaving not like Atreus of Clytemnestra but like Matthew Merrygreek or Diccon of Bedlam. Not only is the effect of the action sometimes overtly comic, as when Pedringano stands with a rope about his neck while

Lorenzo's Page comforts him with an empty box supposedly containing his pardon, but the very methods used are the traditional ones of comic intrigue. Diccon by means of a lost needle sets Dame Chat and Gammer Gurton at loggerheads. Matthew Merrygreek, by means of a mispunctuated letter, effects the same end with Ralph Roister Doister and Dame Custance. The resulting quarrels are trivial, hence in harmony with the trivial means used to foment them; but after Lorenzo's maneuvers with deceptive appointments and an empty box, Serberine and Pedringano are dead. So after the tampering with a letter by Hamlet, Rosencrantz and Guildenstern are dead. And after the manipulation by Iago of a piece of lost needlework (rather than a lost needle), Othello and Desdemona are dead.

The ruse of Atreus in enticing Thyestes into his power is no more elaborate than need be. The difficulty of the end achieved justifies the complexity of the means employed. Such is not the case with the ruses of Lorenzo. He is sufficiently privileged in the state that he might slay Pedringano and Serberine out of hand, with few questions asked, and the intricacy of his methods must be recognized as entertainment for its own sake. Sometimes the later writers of tragedy found their intrigue in source fiction, itself progressive rather than retrospective in narrative method, but they usually complicated this intrigue further, as in the case of *Othello,* or supplemented it with pure invention. The tendency was for the intrigue to become increasingly elaborate from play to play, and from action to action within individual plays. In Marlowe's *Jew of Malta* Barabas disposes of the Christian suitors of his daughter by the relatively simple method of a forged challenge. Although "cunningly perform'd," this action is capped later in the piece when Iacomo is arrested for the murder of the propped-up body of a friar who has already been murdered by Barabas and Ithimore. Marlowe seems here to be letting his villains improve upon the methods of Kyd's Lorenzo.

That Elizabethan tragedy as it evolved is marked by an augmentation of intricacy, owing to a competitive response of playwrights to a taste for intrigue, scarcely needs to be argued. The whole of the plot of *The Revenger's Tragedy* is a multiplication of the devices of Lorenzo in disposing of Serberine and Pedringano, and of Barabas in disposing of Iacomo and the friar. Plays with a strong, simple, and reasonably plausible story line up to a certain point, like Middleton and Rowley's *Changeling* or Webster's *Duchess of Malfi,* will conclude in a welter of trickery, like the grand finale of a pyrotechnical display. Here all former "notable cosenage" will be, so to speak, anthologized. As in the case of Webster's play, the thickening of the plot, the density of the intrigue, is apt to begin where the dependence upon source materials ends. And even the tragedies which are least conspicuous for this trait, such as *King Lear,* are apt to contain at least one sequence in which a clever man manipulates several others to his own destructive ends, employing usually a concrete property, most often a letter, but also a dead body, a weapon, an article of attire, or (alas) a handkerchief.

Thomas Rymer called *Othello* a "bloody farce" and T. S. Eliot has called *The Jew of Malta* a serious "farce." Neither of these estimable critics has quite succeeded in bringing the critical issue into clear focus, and we can understand the reasons why. To the neoclassicist, Elizabethan tragedy seemed so full of excesses and improprieties that his critical energies were fully deployed without the need for observing that tragedy of intrigue is basically a mixed genre. He follows his authorities and objects to the violation of "the unities" in construction, or to the principle of "decorum" in the presentation of character: Iago should not be presented as both a soldier and a sneak! There is little need to meditate upon the comic potential of the intrigue, when comic elements are so often overt, as in the intrusion of the Clown. The modern belletrist is apt to be similarly diverted, but in a different direction and, of course, under greater pressures to express approval. The horrific Barabas, with his self-declared ferocity, seems to him seriocomic in the fashion of mordant caricature quite apart from the nature of the devices he employs. But we must recognize that *The Jew of Malta* and *Othello* are "farces" only in the same way in which most Elizabethan tragedies are, after a manner of speaking, "farces." We are dealing with a pervasive feature of the tragedy of the age with which we must come to terms.

We may as well concede at once that we rarely wish that there were *more* intrigue in Elizabethan tragedy. It is this feature, rather than any violation of "unities" or any overtly comic elements, that makes us a little uneasy under the quizzical glances of admirers of Corneille and Racine. At least in the introductory stages, it is easier to win admiration for serious Elizabethan drama with English history plays like *Edward II* or Roman tragedies like *Julius Caesar*. In these "documentaries" or "semidocumentaries" the playwrights were working under restraints. No one would wish that Shakespeare had elaborated the manner in which Cassius duped Brutus with forged letters, and thus given the episode more substance than it possessed in Plutarch. It is partly the *absence* of intrigue, in the mechanical sense, that gives plays like *Coriolanus* and *Antony and Cleopatra* more innate dignity than plays like *Othello* and *Romeo and Juliet*. They are "classical" in more ways than one. Or in a quite different category of tragedy, the highly original treatments of common domestic transgression, we can often pinpoint the source of our critical discomfiture in the intrigue. The most embarrassing feature of Heywood's *Woman Killed with Kindness* is not its alleged sentimentality, or the intermingling of archaic and modern dramaturgical and didactic devices, but the sequence of scenes in which Master Frankford grows clever with duplicate keys. We wish he had exposed his wife and Wendoll in some other way. He dwindles in tragic dignity not by exercising self-righteously and loquaciously his moral code, but by becoming an intriguer.

Nevertheless, it would be risky to say that Elizabethan tragedy is admirable (on those frequent occasions when it *is* admirable) in spite of its intrigue. This would be a little like saying that certain Elizabethan poems are admirable in spite of their being sonnets. Intrigue in Elizabethan tragedy is so inextricably related to the kind of tragedy it is that to deplore it in general would be to deplore the tragedy in general—to wish it were some other thing. *Macbeth,* with its relative absence of intrigue, seems to me as to so many others a greater tragedy than *Othello,* with its relative abundance of intrigue, but I am by no means sure that intrigue itself, quantitatively considered, explains the difference in stature. *Macbeth* has incomparably the greater theme, with action and language appropriate to the theme. Although intrigue might well have spoiled *Macbeth,* intrigue does not spoil *Othello. The Revenger's Tragedy,* in spite of its widely acclaimed poetry, which proves upon examination to appear only in the first and a few later bravura speeches, strikes me as a bad play—but less because of its intrigue, thickened to the point of coagulation, but because it has so little else to offer. When an Elizabethan tragedy is bad, we seem to recognize the intrigue as a contributory factor, but in last analysis the play is bad not because of the intrigue but because the play is bad.

A generalization that holds here as everywhere is that an ingredient is good to the extent that it synthesizes with other ingredients to form a consistent whole. Intrigue is good to the extent that it is absorbed in the artistic process and serves the artist's end. An instance in which intrigue, featuring all the standard machinery, remains ludicrously *un*absorbed is provided by the episodes involving Bussy, Tamyra, and the interceding Friar in Chapman's *Bussy D'Ambois*. Dryden was inclined to consider *this* play a bloody farce, specifically a "mingle of false poetry and true nonsense." Although Chapman's star is at the moment ascending, it is harder to dispose of Dryden's view of *Bussy* than of Rymer's view of *Othello*.

The most obvious objection to intrigue in tragedy, apart from the fact that it can overtax the constructive skill of the playwright, is that it amuses us, makes us wish momentarily for its success, and creates in us a certain admiration for the intriguer and tolerance for his aims. However, in the case of *Othello* (and *Othello* is the most doubtful case among Shakespeare's major tragedies) our amusement at Iago, and covert admiration, may so involve us in his guilt as to contribute to our final feelings of revulsion against the thing he symbolizes. In the source story, Othello himself was an intriguer: Shakespeare altered that. In *King Lear,* Edmund's manipulation of Gloucester and Edgar by means of his faked letter is no detriment to the play. The intrigue is absorbed by the way it relates to Edmund's character and occasions his revelatory speeches. Great language is a great absorbent, and perhaps we do indeed owe some of the fine Elizabethan dramatic poetry to the gritty stuff it was forced to absorb. More dubious in *King Lear,* so far as artistic success is concerned, is Edgar's intrigue in achieving a trial by combat with Edmund, since deviousness is not a quality of Edgar's character and his ruses are not accompanied by speeches especially powerful. The contrast in effect of these two sequences of action is revealing in the extreme.

It appears that the Elizabethan playwright is most successful in exercising his spell upon us when he is being most true to his own traditions. Although intrigue itself might be new in tragedy, it was not new in its association with evil. The

Vice, a traditional character, was often a comical fellow, but whatever the etymology of his name he symbolized the *vicious;* the awe-inspiring Machiavellian, with his masterful duplicity, merely filled in an ancient outline. One might be entertained by the methods of a Lorenzo, and even admire his cleverness, but such responses were tentative. Men might properly manipulate material things, but not their fellow men; cleverness in human relationships was evil, and should be associated only with characters who will ultimately be rejected. I think we may say that responses which are tentative, provisional, at war with ultimate moral judgment, are not inappropriate to spectators of tragedy, or destructive of ultimate tragic effects. Intrigue could be successfully employed in tragedy by a writer of constructive skill, so long as it was presented as evil in its effects and was associated with evil men.

But Elizabethan tragedy did not confine itself to intrigue in its mischievous aspects. In the comedy from which it borrowed the ingredient, no device was commoner than that of the tricker tricked, the underminer hoisted with his own petard. It was in imitating this feature of comic intrigue that Kyd and later writers muddied the tragic font. Lorenzo we can accept, but not Hieronimo—or Marston's Antonio, or others like him. Cleverness could be pitted against cleverness in comedy; poison could drive out poison, because it was not really poison after all, but only a useful purgative or emetic. In tragedy the poison was deadly, and so must retain its exclusive association with evil. It was possible to introduce a virtuous intriguer successfully, providing his maneuvers, like those of Friar Laurence, were vain or catastrophic, or providing it was made clearly manifest that his intrigues, like his lust for vengeance itself, were eroding away his virtue. But such characters as Hieronimo and Antonio are supposed to retain our approval. They fail to do so, and the plays in which they appear fail to win our approval—at least as tragedy. Whether or not Chapman's Friar in *Bussy D'Ambois* is supposed to retain our approval is a moot point—his devices are certainly as catastrophic in their results as those of Friar Laurence. Vendice in *The Revenger's Tragedy* ends thoroughly corrupted, but owing to his initial and single-minded devotion to trickery, he seems also to have begun corrupted. In neither case is the author's orthodoxy so much in question as his artistic sensibility.

Since all roads seem to lead to *Hamlet,* it would be strange if an essay on intrigue in Elizabethan tragedy failed to do so. If Hamlet was to remain a tragic hero, was to appear more virtuous than not in the eyes of Shakespeare's audience then and now, he could neither take premeditated vengeance nor be a successful intriguer, no matter how intellectually well-equipped. In the antecedent legend (and perhaps in an earlier play by Kyd) that is what Hamlet had been—a successful avenger, a successful intriguer. In Shakespeare's play, his one really successful ruse, disposing of Rosencrantz and Guildenstern, is only passingly reported and plays a negligible part in our total emotional response. His great stroke of intrigue, the mouse-trap play, by which he is so highly elated, resolves itself into an intellectual exercise. It catches the King's conscience but not the King's life. Hamlet meditates the killing of Claudius, but the killing of Claudius is not the fruit of those meditations. Hamlet tries to manipulate men and events, but a divinity shapes his ends. That his hand should slay Claudius is symbolically appropriate, but his hand upon the foil and the cup must be covered by the hand of Providence. Hamlet remains the tragic hero. Such characters as Hieronimo and Antonio are tragic heroes only in the hopeful eyes of their creators. It was an artistic necessity of the case that Hamlet should be so fertile in ideas, so sterile in actions, that upon his intrigues should be graciously conferred a soul-saving futility.

Although *Hamlet* is a success, its success is something of a miracle. The tragedy misses absurdity by a thin margin. Few Elizabethan tragedies are so adroit as Shakespeare's; we admire most of them for individual scenes, characters, and poetic passages, rather than for totality of effect. On the average, Elizabethan comedy, although less memorable in individual scenes, characters, and poetic passages, is more successful in synthesizing its ingredients. From the time of *The Spanish Tragedy* onward the ingredients of Elizabethan tragedy were hard to synthesize.[1] We cannot say that in-

---

[1] My main point does not depend upon the priority of Kyd's play. If intrigue was introduced into popular tragedy by some other play, or by a more gradual process, or through the influence of some earlier mediator between comedy and tragedy such as Italian pastoral "tragicomedy," its significance remains the same. Nevertheless, I believe that Kyd was the innovator, and that the lasting notoriety of *The Spanish Tragedy* was, in some measure, the fruit of its initial novelty. R. B. McKerrow, with whom no one would rashly disagree, questioned the assumption that the slur in Nashe's Epistle to Greene's *Menaphon* (1589) was aimed specifically at Kyd, and Philip Edwards, in his excellent edition for the "Revels" series, dates *The Spanish Tragedy* ca. 1590. But to redirect the interpretation of the whole complex of allusions in Nashe's diatribe to some purely hypothetical playwright or shadowy "group" of playwrights is to place an intolerable strain upon coincidence. After all, Nashe was referring, albeit in the plural, to *a non-university writer of popular "Senecan" plays, successful enough to arouse his ire.* Even at this date it would be hard to name a candidate other than Kyd, and in view of the wrenched allusion to the "Kid in Aesop," along with two allusions to the profession of "Noverint" and the thrusting of "Elisium into hell" (to mention these items only), the case for Kyd becomes quite as strong as the case for Shakespeare as the object of the famous slur in Greene's *Groatsworth of Wit.* Concerning the latter, we can argue that "Shake-scene" is a common type of epithet, like "Tear-throat," and might indicate *any* allegedly bombastic playwright, but in view of the other particularities in the passage (each individually vulnerable), the case for

trigue spoiled Elizabethan tragedy, since particular plays survive to demonstrate the unique and powerful effects achievable with its use, but a tragedy of intrigue, a tragedy cross-bred from comedy, was too difficult for most talents. The playwrights were dealing with *almost* intransigent materials.

Shakespeare becomes too strong to be denied, and few are inclined to deny it. I should say, further, that if Nashe was alluding to Kyd and *The Spanish Tragedy* (where the netherworld geography *is—pace* Edwards— open to cavil), then the play must have been written before the Armada. Absence of allusions to the Armada is not ordinarily a good dating criterion, but in a play with a Spanish scene, and with allusions to English victories over the Spanish, the absence of any allusion to the Armada (prophetic, let us say) would be something of a marvel if that play was written in 1588–89. I do not think that T. W. Baldwin's argument for a date at the beginning of the decade is convincing (*On the Literary Genetics of Shakespere's Plays,* 1959, chap. 6), and I remain loyal to 1586–87. This, coincidentally, is about midpoint of the "five and twenty or thirty" years ago given by Ben Jonson in his induction to *Bartholomew Fair* (1614) as the era of *Andronicus* and "Ieronimo."

*I*N SPEAKING of *The Jew of Malta* as "farce of the old
English humour, the terribly serious, even savage comic
humour, the humour which spent its last breath on the
decadent genius of Dickens . . ."[1] T. S. Eliot set the pitch
for modern Marlovian criticism. We are reminded of Coleridge's remarks about a critical dictum by Milton: "Speaking
of poetry he says (as in a parenthesis), it is 'simple, sensuous,
passionate.' How awful is the power of words! fearful often
in their consequence when merely felt, not understood."[2]
When Eliot called Marlowe's play "farce," he was saying
what, in effect, most previous critics had said[3]—the word
can be "understood." But when he added (as in a parenthesis) that this farce is "terribly serious" in the manner of the
"decadent genius" of Dickens, the words can be "merely
felt." No light is shed on what the farce is terribly serious
about, or in what sense the word "decadent" is used, or if it
applies to the genius of Marlowe as well as to that of Dickens. Indeed we may echo Audrey's plaintive query about
Touchstone's word *poetical:* "I do not know what decadent
is. Is it honest in word and deed? Is it a true thing?"

Reprinted from *Tulane Drama Review*, vol. 8 (1964).

[1] *The Sacred Wood* (London, Methuen, 1928 ed.), p. 92.

[2] *Coleridge's Writings on Shakespeare,* ed. T. Hawkes (New York, 1959),
p. 30.

[3] Charles Lamb, in *Specimens,* 2nd ed. (London, 1813), p. 31, says:
"Barabas is a mere monster brought in with a large painted nose to please
the rabble." Cf. A. H. Bullen, *Works of Christopher Marlowe,* 3 vols. (London, 1885), I, xi; A. W. Ward, *History of English Dramatic Literature,*
3 vols. (London, 1899), I, 338; A. C. Swinburne, *Age of Shakespeare* (London, 1908) p. 5; F. E. Schelling, *Elizabethan Drama,* 2 vols. (Boston, 1908),
I, 233; et al.

Perhaps we should enter the usual caveat, that Mr. Eliot must not be held responsible for the solemn reverberations set off by even his most casual utterances, but in this case we are deterred by the fact that he has contributed greatly to Marlowe's prestige. In the critical climate which has prevailed, poetry which is "terribly serious" is assumed also to be terribly good, and mere mention of "decadent genius" confers honor by association. Praise of Marlowe, universally among bright undergraduates and to some extent among their mentors, is cut to a standard pattern: there is more in Marlowe than meets the innocent eye; his plays form a sequence of interrelated power probes in the cold war of the glorious *one* against the inglorious *many*. Their prevailing mode is ironic. In seeming to castigate sin, in the persons of titanic sinners, Marlowe is really castigating naïve popular notions of sin. The true object of his "savage" humor is the conventional morality of the herd. His plays are all admirably subversive. This view is in harmony with the modern temper, and with the doctrine that good citizens make bad poets since all true art is revolutionary. It is presumably fortified by what the critics think they know about Marlowe's life. The Baines "libel" accusing him of all sins, from smoking to sodomy, and all crimes, from coining to Catholicism (as well as atheism), is no longer kept under wraps, or even cautiously discounted. It is produced with a flourish, like a letter of recommendation.

A fair sample of the "Hail, horrors, hail!" school of criticism appears in an early work by Una Ellis-Fermor: in *The Jew of Malta* "we begin to recognize in Marlowe the man whose trenchant exposure of shams is revealed in the document known as the Baines libel. . . . The dauntless courage and ruthlessness of Machiavelli's doctrines seem at first to have made a strong appeal to Marlowe; and in *The Jew of Malta,* which may have been written in the first burst of this enthusiasm, he invests him with a certain poetic splendour, the splendour of the Satanist warring on behalf of cold logic against a world-order of superstition, sentimentalism, and hypocrisy."[4] This earnest rhetoric (richer in warm passion than "cold logic") may have embarrassed its author a little as she ripened with her generation, but it expresses a view still widely held—that the play which purports to be an exposé of Machiavellianism was actually written in a "burst" of enthusiasm for it.

Tucker Brooke, an editor and critic of an older persuasion, became aware that the bright Marlowe whom he had taken to his heart in his guileless youth was darkening before his eyes. In his latest conspectus, he offered some resistance— "It is unfashionable but just to assert the abstention from impure suggestion in all Marlowe's original work"—but he felt obliged to give at least a nod to the business of *trenchant exposure of shams*—"Better a true Turk, he [Marlowe] says, or a consistent Jew, than a faithless and time-serving Christian."[5] Actually Marlowe says nothing of the kind, at least in *The Jew of Malta,* but even if he had done so, his would not have been a lonely voice raised in an "age of bigotry." The disparity between the profession of Christianity and the practice of Christians was a very familiar theme, and no didactic device was commoner than instancing, as a reproach, the superior virtues of particular non-Christians. In Robert Wilson's *Three Ladies of London,* a popular play already in print when Marlowe began to write, Gerontus, a worthy Jew, forgives a debt rather than let Mercadorus, a contemptible Christian, effect its legal cancellation by swearing the following oath: "I, Mercadorus, do utterly renounce before all the world my duties to my Prince, my honour to

[4] *Christopher Marlowe* (London, 1927), pp. 89, 97.
[5] *A Literary History of England,* ed. A. C. Baugh (New York, 1948), pp. 513, 515.

my parents, and my good wil to my cuntry. . . . Futhermore,
I protest and sweare to be true to [Turkey] during life, and
thereupon I forsake my Christian faith." Observing the
horror of the virtuous Jew, and his generous self-sacrifice, the
Turkish judge observes that "Jewes seeke to excell in Chris-
tiantie, and Christians in Jewisness."[6]

Now I would not claim, although the author of *The Jew
of Malta* must have known *The Three Ladies of London*
(and may even have taken some hints from it, since Gerontus is possessed of "Diamondes, Rubyes, Emerodes, Safiors,
Opalles, Onacles, Jasinkes, Aggates, Turkasis, and almost all
kinde of precious stones"), that in electing to portray a
properly evil Jew instead of an improperly good one, a conservative Marlowe was rebuking a radical Wilson. Both were
abiding by standard conventions. The true distinction between them is that Marlowe was a master of language, as
Wilson was not, and a far superior theatrical craftsman. Its
theatrical mastery, its *showmanship,* is the most remarkable
thing about this play by a young man who had been spend-
ing his time, not as an actor like Wilson, but as an academic
at Cambridge. It is studded with plot devices and verbal
routines (double talk, cross-purpose dialogue, patterned
interruption, satirical asides, etc.) which passed on as models
to later playwrights. Of course we cannot be sure how much
Marlowe himself owed to the lost repertories of the Theatre
and Curtain during the first decade of their existence, 1576–
1586.

The limited objective of the present essay is to question the
conception of Marlowe as iconoclast. My point is that he was
not (because he was temperamentally disqualified) either a
"Satanist" or an adept at portraying corruption. The writers
who emerged a decade or so later—Jonson, Marston, Middle-

---

[6] *Three Ladies of London* (1584), sig. FI.

ton, Tourneur, and others—leave him at the post in this regard, and his plays, as compared with some of theirs, belong to an "uncontaminated springtime."

We do not know when *The Jew of Malta* was written, or in what form it stood when it left Marlowe's hands. It is better to admit this fact than to base critical judgments upon a hypothetical chronology, or upon selected portions of the play as alone representative of a hypothetical "original." The only existing text was sponsored on the Caroline stage and in print by Thomas Heywood in 1633, forty years after Marlowe's death. My own view is that the play was written early rather than late in the poet's brief career, and that the existing text is a true version slightly cut. Like *Doctor Faustus,* it is something of a "primitive" in its technique; its structure is clearly derived from the expanding Tudor interludes. Although twenty-three characters are represented, besides an unspecified number of Knights, Officers, and Bashaws, few are together upon the stage at any one time, so that the play could be performed by a rump troupe. *Three* Jews are twice referred to as "multitudes," and when Barabas (now Governor of Malta) prepares his death trap for the Turks, he himself appears "with a hammer above, very busy." There is maximum fluidity in the treatment of time and place. Intrigues are projected and completed almost simultaneously; and characters move from place to place, including in and out of houses, without interrupting their dialogue. This means that there was much pantomimic action upon a universalized platform. At one point Barabas drinks a potion like that supplied by Friar Laurence to Juliet, is brought in apparently dead, is tossed over the walls of Malta, returns to life, and offers aid to the Turkish besiegers—all this in continuous action requiring only twenty lines of dialogue.

The act divisions have no discernible structural significance, and the difference in length of the present five "acts" may provide our best clue to the degree of deterioration marring the existent text. It seems likely that originally the play was simply sliced into five approximately equal parts, and that the present brevity of the last three slices means that cutting has occurred in them, with occasional substitution of utilitarian patches of prose for original passages of verse. This does not mean, of course, that *all* the prose passages are redactions. Assuming that such is what has occurred, it follows that not much has been lost. The play is 2410 lines long, as compared with Marlowe's longest play (and most perfect text), *Edward the Second,* which is 2640 lines. I should guess that about 100 lines have been cut in each of the last two "acts," a little more in the third. I should also guess that the cutting was done early in the stage career of the play, and not necessarily by Heywood. Certainly Heywood did not serve as "censor." In some of his own inoffensive plays there is more "impure suggestion" than appears in *The Jew of Malta.* Although the first part of the play has the greater literary interest, since in it ideas and emotions are given fuller poetic expression, we cannot conclude that it alone is representative of Marlowe. Any cutting or other form of modification probably only accentuated a characteristic which already existed—as "action" progressively tended to crowd out discursive speech. Long ago, Henry Hallam shrewdly attributed this feature of the play to a general tendency in Elizabethan tragedies of blood. Although there is more and more sacrifice of poetic to theatrical opportunity as the play proceeds, *The Jew of Malta* is from the beginning preeminently a "stage piece." I feel sure that the ethical, if not in equal measure the aesthetic, qualities of Marlowe's original play are fairly represented in the text we have. In any case my argument is built squarely upon it.

Although our interest (as was that of Marlowe) is primarily in Barabas, we should not lose sight of the other characters or see them only through Barabas' eyes. The idea that he is depicted as an honestly wicked character in a dishonestly wicked world is erroneous. Barabas is not honestly wicked, but flagrantly self-righteous, and the world of Malta is not depicted as wicked at all. In fact its governor, Ferneze, would have been greeted by an Elizabethan audience with warm moral approval. That we cannot endorse this approval is beside the point. Ferneze exacts large fines from Barabas and his co-religionists, but in a society like London's, where men had recently been burned for being the wrong kind of Christians, no one would have been shocked by a society like Malta's where men were fined for being Jews. Ferneze provides a choice: any Jew who becomes a Christian will share the Christian immunity from fine; otherwise he will pay half his estate. The offer would have seemed not only just but generous. All of the estate of Barabas is confiscated when he proves momentarily defiant, but this does not mean that Ferneze is portrayed as tyrannical. The penalty was named in the original stipulation, and although Barabas immediately recants, he must pay the penalty. The Elizabethans loved these illogical "legalisms"—contracts so literally interpreted that all parties are stymied, oaths binding even upon conscienceless villains, predictions filled in every trivial detail, etc. In the present play a friar, although something of a scalawag, feels bound by the secrecy of the confessional, even though it is protecting the hated Barabas. But, one may say, Ferneze fails to use the extracted fines for their intended purpose, to pay the Turkish tribute. Again quite proper. Why should Christian Malta remain in Turkish thrall when it becomes militarily feasible to do otherwise? In the end Ferneze tricks the tricker, Barabas, and at the same time, although more humanely than the latter would have done, also expunges the Turks, so that Malta is again in Christian control. He is quite the hero.

The modern error is to accept Barabas' own definition of "policy," and thus to admit no distinction between the "policy" of Ferneze on behalf of Malta, that of Calymath on behalf of the Turkish Grand Signior, that of Del Bosco on behalf of the Spanish Emperor—and that of Barabas on behalf of himself:

> Nay, let 'em combat, conquer, and kill all
> So they spare me, my daughter, and my wealth.
>
> (I.i. 150–151)

Barabas' exception of his daughter (whom he himself soon kills) is only privisional, and although he expresses pride in his race, he admits no obligation even to fellow Jews. It was only this exclusively self-interested "policy" that would have been viewed as wholly reprehensible, "Machiavellian." To suppose that everyone in the play is tarred with the same brush is to ignore the direction of the action. There is, whether we like it or not, a hierarchy of social acceptability and privilege postulated in the play, with the Knights of Malta at the top, the Jews at the bottom, and the Spaniards and Turks in between. This structure is nicely honored in what finally happens to the leaders of its various segments, with Ferneze triumphing and Barabas boiling, and with Del Bosco successful in his mission and Calymath unsuccessful (but at least saved from the hot cauldron). One may say with justice that the schematization is ethically crude, but this is a different thing from saying it does not exist or is being held up to ridicule. There are, of course, worlds within worlds, a disapproved Catholicism incorporated in an approved Christianity, so that not all the non-Jewish Maltese are free from stain; but to be simultaneously "pro" and "anti" in religious sentiment presented no difficulties to the Elizabethan mind.

Granted that Marlowe is more interested in the morally

black Barabas than in his morally neutral or mixed milieu, what is the nature of that interest? I should say that it is primarily that of the popular entertainer; and that we shall get nearer the truth about the play if we ourselves are less "terribly serious" about it, and think a little less in terms of moral philosophy and a little more in terms of native sports. There was bear-baiting, bull-baiting, and, their theatrical equivalent, devil-baiting. Behind the latter lies a long tradition, with the "Vice" figures of the interludes bustling aggressively and triumphantly among men until their final preordained discomfiture. The aggression of the Vice figure was not originally deadly. He pestered by placing boards under the earth where the farmer must dig, or by setting neighbors at loggerheads, but he succeeded in killing neither bodies nor souls, so that in a sense he was frustrated—"baited" —even before his final downfall. (The last was sometimes absentmindedly neglected by the interludists.) The appeal was primarily comic. The comic action persisted, elaborated after the example of classical comedy of intrigue, even when its results became deadly and gave us the peculiarly mixed quality of a certain type of Elizabethan "tragedy."

In Marlowe's play the devil is baited in the form of a Machiavellian Jew. If the sport was to be any fun, the "baitee" must seem dangerous. In the game ring, an amiable bear or a listless bear would not do—the game masters must occasionally be clawed and the bulldogs gored and tossed. The same principle applied in the theatre. The devil figure must have his ups and downs, so that an audience might greet the "ups" with glee, "laughing all in one voice at any notable act of cozenage," and the "downs" with pious approval. Marlowe is not mocking the popular audience in *The Jew of Malta,* but conspiring hand-and-glove with it. He supplied the best devil-figure thus far conceived—in his agile-minded, arrogant, ruthless, lethal Barabas.

But observe the limitations of this monster of wickedness. He stacks up heaps of wealth (obtained by far from sordid means), and he kills people. That about covers it. Although an expert casuist and liar, and a marvelously ingenious contriver, the endproduct of his villainy is more notable for quantity than quality. His competence extends only to *means*, not to *ways* of sinning. He kills people in heaps, but is most remiss in administering mental and physical agony. This limitation is extended to his Turkish instrument, Ithimore, whose boasted achievement in torture reminds us of a schoolboy's prank with itching powder:

> Once at Jerusalem where the pilgrims kneeled,
> I strewèd powder on the marble stones,
> And therewithal their knees would rankle so
> That I have laughed a-good to see the cripples
> Go limping home to Christendom on stilts.
> (ii.iii. 205–209)

Barabas' own masterpiece of cruelty, the boiling cauldron prepared for Calymath and his bashaws but destined for himself, operates with somewhat less than horrifying efficiency:

> But now begins the extremity of heat
> To pinch me with intolerable pangs.
> Die, life! Fly, soul! Tongue, curse thy fill, and die!
> (v.v.87–89)

Could Barabas have read Marston's *Antonio's Revenge*, Tourneur's *Revenger's Tragedy,* Webster's *White Devil,* or a score of similar plays, he would have learned right *ways* to make men die.

Could Barabas have read the city comedies of the Stuart and Caroline stage, he would have learned right *ways* of hoarding up filthy lucre. It never even occurs to him to prostitute his lovely daughter: he is mindful of Abigail's chastity when actually using her as a decoy; the grounds of the intrigue at this point are the honorable intentions of her rival lovers. The whole book of sexual criminality is closed to Barabas—and as a sensualist he fails to compete. Again the limitation is extended to his Turkish associate. When Ithimore addresses Bellamira in the brothel (itself about as sexy as a surgery), this is his most lubricious speech:

> I'll be thy Jason, thou my golden fleece.
> Where painted carpets o'er the meads are hurled,
> And Bacchus' vineyards overspread the world,
> Where woods and forests go in goodly green,
> I'll be Adonis; thou shalt be Love's queen.
> The meads, the orchards, and the primrose lanes,
> Instead of sedge, and reed, bear sugar canes.
> Thou in those groves, by Dis above,
> Shall live with me, and be my love.
>
> (iv. iv. 86–94)

Sugar canes!—it is as if one were invoking the fleshly delights of peanut brittle. Compare this speech with the amatory and gustatory visions of Jonson's Sir Epicure Mammon. There are in Marlowe's play some naughty quips, usually involving the interest of the friars in the nuns, but they are few in number and faint in impact. The one touching Barabas himself—

> *Friar Barnardine. Thou hast committed—*
> *Barabas.* Fornication? But that
>   Was in another country, and besides
>   The wench is dead.
>
> (iv. i. 40–43)

probably is no more than a joke on the speaker's age and present sexual incapacity, but because of Marlowe's way with words, it has a haunting quality which has suggested various things to various critics (although I hope not necrophilia).

The heady combination of lust and bloodshed, eroticism *cum* the macabre, does not appear in *The Jew of Malta* or elsewhere in Marlowe.

The truth is that Barabas (and that means Marlowe, since the latter necessarily "identified" with his central character, and thought as "wickedly" as he could) is essentially innocentminded. The actual language of the play, the *poetry,* closely and candidly scrutinized, provides the best proof of the fact. The blackest speeches pale to light gray when placed by comparable ones in the plays of certain of Marlowe's successors. I shall confine myself to a single illustration—dictated by Eliot's extension of his statement quoted at the beginning of this essay. Again the words of no content ("very serious") are used, together with additional words of no content ("very different"): "It [the humor of *The Jew of Malta*] is the humour of that very serious (but very different) play, *Volpone*." That *Volpone* is not the same play as *The Jew of Malta* is such a certainty that "very different" must have some additional meaning; perhaps if we knew what that meaning was, everything in the critique would prove enlightening as well as imposing. I shall quote, side by side, Barabas' opening address to his gold and jewels, and Volpones opening address to *his* gold and jewels:

> *Barabas*. Give me the merchants of the Indian mines
> That trade in metal of the purest mold,
> The wealthy Moor that in the eastern rocks
> Without control can pick his riches up
> And in his house heap pearl like pebble-stones,
> Receive them free and sell them by the weight.
> Bags of fiery opals sapphires, amethysts,
> Jacinths, hard topaz, grass-green emeralds,
> Beauteous rubies sparkling diamonds,
> And seld-seen costly stones of so great price

As one of them, indifferently rated
And of a carat of this quantity,
May serve in peril of calamity
To ransom great kings from captivity—
This is the ware wherein consists my wealth.
And thus methinks should men of judgment frame
Their means of traffic from the vulgar trade,
And as their wealth increaseth, so enclose
Infinite riches in a little room.

(I. i. 19–37)

Volpone. Good morning to the day; and next, my gold!
Open the shrine that I may see my saint.
Hail the world's soul, and mine! More glad than is
The teeming earth to see the longed-for sun
Peep through the horns of the celestial Ram,
Am I, to view thy splendor darkening his;
That lying here, amongst my other hoards,
Show'st like a flame by night, or like the day
Struck out of chaos, where all darkness fled
Unto the center. O thou son of Sol,
But brighter than thy father, let me kiss,
With adoration, thee, and every relic
Of sacred treasure in this blessed room.
Well did wise poets by thy glorious name
Title that age which they would have the best,
Thou being the best of things, and far transcending
All style of joy in children, parents, friends,
Or any other waking dream on earth.
Thy looks when they to Venus did ascribe,
They should have giv'n her twenty thousand cupids,
Such are thy beauties and our loves!

(I i. 1–21)

Now Barabas, in speaking of his wealth, does actually speak
of his wealth, its strangeness, beauty, and power, at the same

time making a practical point about space-saving. (He had begun by making a similar point about time-saving: "what a trouble 'tis to count this trash," i.e., mere silver.) Wealth, as the idea of it is here invoked, remains one of the Aristotelian *good things,* like health, unsicklied o'er with the pale cast of moralistic brooding. This is not "dirty money"— soiled either by baseness of acquisition or by invidious comparison with higher human values—but quite clean money. One would like to have it. Volpone, in contrast, is not speaking of wealth at all, but is invoking, with more than a hint of blasphemy, the idea of false values, the worship of the golden calf, and the corruption of the world. Putting it briefly, the *poetry* of Barabas' speech expresses aspiration, the *poetry* of Volpone's, perversion.

Considering the fact that Barabas had just been introduced to the audience by "Machevil" (and we should not be oblivious to the pun) as the incarnation of evil, it would have been appropriate if his opening speech had something of the flavor of Volpone's. Why does it not? The reason, I think, is that Marlowe's mind did not run naturally in evil channels, that he had little imaginative affinity with corruption; and whereas he could *invent* a limited repertory of wicked things for a Barabas to do, he could not *imagine* the appropriate things for such a doer to think. To some extent this is true also of his other great transgressors, notably Doctor Faustus; they may shock but they never disgust; there is a disparity between what they do and what they seem to be, between role and atmosphere. We should not conclude that their creator is "up to something"—that he is consciously making his sinners ingratiating, that he is a cunning propagandist on the side of the fallen angels. True, Marlowe, is *in them,* but we should be a little more discriminating in defining what part of Marlowe is in what part of his creations, in identifying his essence.

It is something very youthful, very pure, and more than a little beautiful. The word *decadent* should not be used even in the remotest connection with it. We should not willingly trade it for something more intellectually and morally weighty, more "terribly serious," but also much less rare.

PART II

*A*FTER remarking that Sir Edmund Chambers, "the very pink of orthodoxy and paragon of caution," declines to recognize any date earlier than 1590-91 for Shakespeare's extant work, F. P. Wilson continues, "The fact is that the chronology of Shakespeare's earliest plays is so uncertain that it has no right to harden into an orthodoxy, and perhaps we should do better to say that by 1592 he had certainly written *Henry VI* (all three parts), *Richard III, The Comedy of Errors,* probably *Titus Andronicus* and possibly *The Taming of the Shrew,* and that the earliest of these may have been written as early as 1588.[1] The statement, like the delightful book in which it appears, is liberal in intention, but it is tinged with the orthodoxy which it gently rebukes. As it proceeds from "certainly" to "probably" to "possibly," still excluding *Love's Labor's Lost,* it seems to sound an irrevocable doom. At the beginning of the eighteenth century *Love's Labor's Lost* was considered Shakespeare's first (and worst) play. At the end of the nineteenth, although "worst" was no longer a permissible word in Shakespearean commentary, the best Shakespeare scholars were convinced that "the first draft of the comedy must have been written when the author was a youth."[2] These "best scholars" were

From *Studies in English Drama Presented to Baldwin Maxwell,* ed. C. B. Woods and C. A. Zimansky, *Philological Quarterly,* vol. 41, no. 1 (January 1962).

[1] F. P. Wilson, *Marlowe and the Early Shakespeare* (Oxford, 1953), p. 113. The author on p. 121 passingly refers to *Love's Labor's Lost* as coming "soon" after the early plays and parodying their "artifices of style."

[2] H. H. Furness, New Variorum edition (1904), p. 337, quoting William Winter (1891).

F. J. Furnivall, presiding genius of the New Shakspere Society; F. G. Fleay, indefatigable analyst of versification and sundry clues; A. W. Ward, leading historian of the English drama; and Sir Sidney Lee, Shakespeare's "definitive" biographer. Their date for the play was 1587-1590. "To *Love's Labour's Lost,*" said Lee decisively, "may reasonably be assigned priority in point of time of all Shakespeare's dramatic productions."[3] This was the *old* orthodoxy. With equal decisiveness the best scholars of the present century have dated the play in the midnineties as one of the lyrical group. This is the *new* orthodoxy.

Orthodoxies are begotten of orthodoxies; firm stands on debatable issues are often assumed, at least in part, in reaction to preceding stands. Old opinions are recognizable as articles of belief. New opinions are easily mistaken for fact. Perhaps it is safest to remain moderate in faith.

One of the forces which have led to the redating of *Love's Labor's Lost* is the twentieth-century tendency to upgrade plays formerly regarded as unworthy, such as *Titus Andronicus* and *Troilus and Cressida. Love's Labor's Lost* is another brand snatched from the burning. In the eighteenth and nineteenth centuries it was considered poor and early. It is no longer considered poor, and hence (small value in this *hence*) no longer considered early. Scholars have insisted, and rightly, that it is poor only if judged by standards inapplicable to it. It is a coterie play, a "courtly" play, and stands naturally in contrast with the popular plays which have established in our minds the Shakespearean norm. So far so good. It is when we ask how a coterie play came to be written during the single interval when there were no coterie theatres (1591-1598) that we detect a thinning of the

---

[3] *Life of Shakespeare* (London, 1898), p. 50. The statement remains unchanged in subsequent editions; cf. ed. 1917, p. 102, and others.

ice. "Doubtless," says Kittredge, "the play was written for performance at court or at some great house."[4] The view is shared by Chambers ("suggests a courtly rather than a popular audience")[5] and by the two most ambitious of its modern editors, Dover Wilson ("written for a private performance in the house of some grandee")[6] and Richard David ("written for private performance in court circles").[7] This is a meager sampling of current affirmations—which are usually supplemented with suggestions of particular occasions in particular great houses where the play might have seen its birth.

Love's Labor's Lost thus joins the swelling list of plays for which private auspices of production are hypothesized: Midsummer Night's Dream for a noble wedding (with various weddings deemed appropriate), Merry Wives for an installation fête of the Order of the Garter (with several installations available), Troilus and Cressida for a feast at the inns of court (there were four inns and many feasts), and so on. The trouble is that there is nothing to support any of these hypotheses except the other hypotheses, now functioning as ghostly precedents. There is no supporting external evidence to prove that any regular play performed by any regular company, juvenile or adult, was originally written for a special occasion during the whole reign of Elizabeth and lifetime of Shakespeare. This total absence of evidence would be rather remarkable if such plays were as common in fact as they have become in theory. They are the kind of thing (as witness the entertainments offered during Elizabeth's progresses, and the masques at James's court) such as would have left records—in household accounts, in contemporary

---

[4] Shakespeare: Complete Works (Boston, 1936), p. 193.
[5] William Shakespeare, A Study of Facts and Problems (Oxford, 1933), I, 338.
[6] New Cambridge edition (1923), p. xxxiv.
[7] New Arden edition (1951), p. 1.

gossip, and on title pages. Instead we have records like the following: "I have sent and bene all thys morning huntyng for players, Juglers & Such kinde of Creatures, but fynde them harde to finde, wherfore Leavinge notes for them to seeke me, Burbage ys come, & Sayes ther ys no new playe that the quene hath not seene, but they have Revyved an olde one, Cawled *Loves Labore lost,* which for wytt & mirthe he sayes will please her excedingly. And Thys ys apointed to be playd to Morowe night at my Lord of Sowthamptons, unless yow send a wrytt to Remove the Corpus Cum Causa to your howse in Strande. Burbage ys my messenger Ready attendyng your pleasure."[8] The tone of this epistle conveys much truth about the theatrical world of the Elizabethans, who did not accord their great drama quite the respect that we do. That they were willing to accept for their private occasions plays from the regular repertories is proven by *many* records, of the royal court, the inns of court, and the "great houses." The Essex faction, even when in need of a propaganda piece in 1601, settled for *Richard II,* a back number in the Chamberlain's Men's repertory. In 1599 Henslowe paid Dekker £2 "for the eande of Fortewnates for the corte."[9] He had already paid Dekker £7 for working over the play, which had been in some form or other part of the Admiral's Men's repertory since at least 1596. A company was willing to invest £2 in presumed royal gratitude, charging the sum against the modest fee they would receive for the court performance, but to buy and mount an entire play would have been another matter. And there is little to suggest that the court, the inns of court, or the great houses would have been willing to under-

[8] Letter of Sir Walter Cope to Robert Cecil, Lord Cranborne, endorsed "1604" apparently for January 1605; see Chambers, *William Shakespeare,* II, 332. (I am assuming that the letter refers to the performance noted in Chambers, p. 331.)

[9] *Henslowe's Diary,* ed. W. W. Greg (London, 1904–1908), I, 116.

write an entire production by professional actors, whose regular wares were available at fixed rates. Moreover, the writing and rehearsing of a play was a considerable undertaking, then as now, requiring more time than was normally available during preparations for a party. It does not follow that there was never a play ad hoc, but in view of the difficulties and the absence of records, it is clear that they could not have been common—not common enough surely to supply an easy explanation for the puzzling characteristics of every puzzling play. The burden of proof rests with those who resort to the explanation.

Love's Labor's Lost was duly performed for Queen Anne in 1605 after Burbage made his suggestion. It had probably been performed before Queen Elizabeth under similar circumstances before its publication in 1598—"As it was presented before her Highnes this last Christmas. Newly corrected and augmented By W. Shakespere." The best scholars of the old orthodoxy naïvely read "newly corrected and augmented" to mean that Shakespeare had refurbished a play for the court performance much as Dekker had refurbished *Old Fortunatus*. Several duplicate passages in the text indicate cancels printed in error, and hence revision. The twentieth century has learned to read bibliographical evidence more subtly. The duplicate passages indicate revision in the course of original composition rather than in working over old matter; and the "newly corrected and augmented" may mean that there had been a "bad quarto" (now lost) just as there had been a bad quarto of *Romeo and Juliet* before the publication of the good quarto of 1599. True the latter reads "newly corrected, augmented, and amended," a slightly different thing, but we may admit the virtue of the suggestion.

Oddly enough, however, the new bibliographical findings do not in the least affect the old assumption that the 1598 quarto of *Love's Labor's Lost* represents an early play reworked, although they have seemed to do so to the finders. The duplicate passages indicate alterations during original composition, but only during composition of those parts of the play where they occur. Those parts *in toto* may be revisions, and as a matter of fact there is evidence (generally conceded) of revision of a different kind—structural revision, such as continues to suggest what the duplicate passages used to suggest. And although there may have been a "bad quarto," there is no reason to assume that it resembled the bad quarto of *Romeo and Juliet*, a debased version of the extant text. Since we are only hypothesizing it anyway, we may as well hypothesize something more on the order of *A Shrew, King Leir*, or the *Troublesome Reign*, or even a *good* version of an earlier form of the present play. Even a bad quarto precisely like that of *Romeo and Juliet* would not cancel the possibility that the text it debased had itself been "newly corrected and augmented." That the 1598 quarto of *Love's Labor's Lost* was printed from the author's draft seems to me to have been proved,[10] but this draft may well have incorporated whole sheets from an earlier draft. Whereas the new findings do not really affect former assumptions, they seem (quaintly) to have prompted a compromise—to the effect that there *was* an early version but *less early* than formerly assumed. Perhaps it seemed wasteful to offer new data without offering new conclusions.

Of incalculable effect in the dating controversy has been Warburton's fatal surmise of 1747 that Holofernes in *Love's Labor's Lost* represents John Florio. Commentators worried this bone for a century and a half, then suddenly filled the air with dust in digging up rival bones. Warburton spoke with irritating certainty, and he was no intellectual giant; it is fitting that his statement should have aroused contempt in

[10] This is the view of W. W. Greg, *The Shakespeare First Folio* (Oxford, 1955), pp. 219–223.

our times, but one wishes that the contempt had been directed at his mental processes rather than at their product. He should be blamed for the nature of his laboring rather than for his mouse. To him the fact that part of A resembled part of B meant that A was B. It means nothing of the kind, but neither do similar equations mean that A was really C or D or E or F, and so on endlessly. Actually, the suggestion that Holofernes is Florio is no worse, and considerably better, than most rival suggestions. None of the characters in *Love's Labor's Lost* resemble in other than a generic fashion (and not very much in that) any of the actual persons with whom they have been identified: King Philip, Bishop Cooper, Northumberland, Southampton, Perez, Lyly, Chapman, Ralegh, Harriot, Harvey, Nashe, etc. Not one of the episodes in the play resembles even generically the actual episodes in the Marprelate and Harvey-Nashe controversy, the Southampton marriage negotiations, the association of Ralegh with suspect intellectuals, etc. The methods used by the expounders of "topicalities" differ only in degree of recklessness from the methods used by Eva Turner Clark in proving that *Love's Labor's Lost* was written by the Earl of Essex in 1578[11] or Abel Lefranc in proving that the earl was not Oxford but Derby.[12] The method is not that of beginning with a mystery and finding a clue, but of beginning with a clue and finding a mystery. None of the advocates of the rival interpretations have been able to convince one another, and all of them collectively should be unable to convince anyone who has passed an elementary course in logic.

So much in way of truth. Immediately we must recognize that most of the expounders have done sound scholarly work of other kinds, and that their work even in this kind is

---

[11] *The Satirical Comedy, Love's Labor's Lost* (New York, 1933).
[12] *Sous le masque de William Shakespeare* (Paris, 1918–1919), II, 87–100.

published under respectable auspices.[13] *Love's Labor's Lost* seems to act upon them as catnip acts upon perfectly sane cats, and possibly the fault lies in the play itself. Although its situations are conventional, there is a curious open-endedness about them which sends the fancies groping, and although all its jokes are explicable as jokes, some of them are so execrably bad as to create *hope* for ulterior meanings. And indeed there are some few phrases associated with the persons and topics adduced. Shakespeare used the idiom of his day. There must be other phrases associated with other topics which happily lie too deeply buried for exploitation. Catch phrases derived from current events do not mean that the writing where they occur has to do with those events, and if the phrases appear in revised writing, they tell us nothing of original date and source of inspiration. Yet the sheer weight of the discussion of "topicalities," most of which date 1590–1595, has created a sentiment or "climate of opinion" in favor of a date of original composition in the midnineties, even among those who reject the specific findings of the expounders. Perhaps they are unconsciously influenced by the dubious principle that where there is smoke there must be fire, or perhaps they are simply too charitable to remain impervious to so much earnest endeavor. Still a heap of fallacies has no more authority than any one of the fallacies comprising the heap; otherwise Shakespeare would surely

[13] The most conspicuous modern works on the "topicalities" since the speculations of F. G. Fleay, Arthur Acheson, and J. M. Robertson have been: Austin K. Gray, "The Secret of *Love's Labour's Lost*," *PMLA*, 39 (1924), 581–611; John Dover Wilson, *Love's Labour's Lost*, New Cambridge edition (1923); Francis A. Yates, *A Study of Love's Labour's Lost* (Cambridge, 1936); Muriel C. Bradbrook, *The School of Night* (Cambridge, 1936). More conservative but bearing in the same direction is Rupert Taylor's *The Date of Love's Labour's Lost* (New York, 1932). A general endorsement seems to be given the speculative school by Richard David in his New Arden edition (1951).

be Bacon. The twentieth-century discussion of the "true meaning" of *Love's Labor's Lost,* heretical though it has seemed to conservative scholars such as Chambers and Kittredge, has nevertheless influenced their new orthodoxy in dating the play ca. 1595.

It is time for more positive considerations. Anyone who maintains that the original version of the play was written between 1592 and 1597, and probably about 1595, must supply satisfactory answers to several questions. First of all, why does the play contain 228 lines of verse like the following?

> *Princess.* What plume of feathers is he that indited this letter?
> What vane? What weathercock? Did you ever hear better?
> *Boyet.* I am much deceived but I remember the style.
> *Princess.* Else your memory is bad, going o'er it erewhile.
> *Boyet.* This Armado is a Spaniard that keeps here in court,
> A phantasime, a Monarcho, and one that makes sport
> To the Prince and his bookmates.
> *Princess.*   Thou fellow, a word:
> Who gave you this letter?
> *Costard.*   I told you—my Lord. (IV.i.93–100)

Nothing resembling such verse appears in *Richard II, Midsummer Night's Dream,* or *Romeo and Juliet,* the plays of the lyrical group. Indeed verse of this kind appears in quantity in only one other place in Shakespeare,[14] in act I, scene iii of *The Comedy of Errors,* and there it has been viewed, at least by some, as a fossil of some quite early anterior version of the play.[15] It is hard to believe that, having adapted so perfectly to his purpose blank verse and the heroic couplet in the plays

---

[14] There are a few quite brief patches of doggerel in *Two Gentlemen of Verona* and *The Taming of the Shrew;* elsewhere in Shakespeare's acknowledged plays there is only a scattered couplet or two, serving a specific whimsical purpose.

[15] Allison Gaw, "The Evolution of the *Comedy of Errors*," *PMLA,* 41 (1926), 620–666.

of the lyrical group (and in parts of *Love's Labor's Lost* itself), Shakespeare would have relapsed to doggerel and considered it appropriate for the witty exchanges of royal and noble speakers. Dover Wilson, Chambers, and Kittredge have all spoken, justly, of the poetic facility of *Love's Labor's Lost* and the maturity of its blank verse. This means that they have been looking at less inconvenient passages than the one sampled above. Looking at such passages, A. W. Ward spoke of the "peculiarities, not to say crudities, of its versification,"[16] and W. J. Courthope of the resemblance to "the lumbering metre of the Moralities."[17]

Tumbling measures had been characteristic of the school drama of Nicholas Udall (*Ralph Roister Doister,* ca. 1553); they persist in the chapel drama of Richard Edwardes (*Damon and Pythias,* 1565); and as late as 1581–1584 appear in Peele's *Arraignment of Paris* performed by the Children of the Chapel while based in their theatre at Blackfriars. In fact the latter play, mingling as it does quatrains, heroic couplets, blank verse, and so on, with old-fashioned doggerel, provides the nearest analogy we have to the commixture of measures in *Love's Labor's Lost.* Lyly's plays for the boy companies in the eighties were written in prose, but one can easily imagine other plays for these companies continuing in the manner of Peele and persevering in the use of tumbling measures until the end of the decade. Those who can just as easily imagine these measures being used by Shakespeare in a play written for the Chamberlain's Men in the midnineties should come to the assistance of the stubborn-minded. Chambers suggests that he was "experimenting" with their comic effect in *The Comedy of Errors.*[18] Was he still "experimenting" in 1595? Charlton's explanation does not strike me as helpful. In

---

[16] *History of English Dramatic Literature* (London, 1875), I, 372.

[17] *History of English Poetry* (London, 1895–1910), IV (1903), 83.

[18] Chambers, *William Shakespeare,* I, 308.

dismissing the doggerel as indication of an early date, he says "it is somewhat as if Shakespeare's metrical level at the period of *Hamlet* should be judged by reckoning the Player's declamation and the play within the play as the normal type."[19] But this is precisely my point. The tumbling measures in *Love's Labor's Lost* appear in no extraneous portions of the play, but in exactly those portions where we should expect to find verse of the "normal type."

My second question has to do with why Shakespeare should perversely have hit upon such a constellation of character names as "Navarre," "Berowne," "Longaville," and "Dumaine" for the members of his whimsical semi-Arcadian "academe" if the selection was made at any time later than August 1589. Before that date the choice was logical enough. The family of Navarre ruled in a small kingdom pleasingly associated in English minds with continental Protestantism, and the other names belonged to French noble houses important enough to be linked fictitiously with the "King of Navarre" in some never-never time when his name was Ferdinand, son of Charles. But after August 1589 the case was different. By edict of the deceased Henry III, the actual "Navarre" was now King of France, engaged in a death-struggle with the League. The struggle was of crucial concern to the English. Three thousand English levies from London died in Navarre's cause in its first year. In 1591 the Earl of Essex was sent to assist him by besieging Rouen. In April of that year Essex banqueted with Navarre, Biron, and Longaville. The latter two were no longer just any French lords, but Navarre's most important generals. "Dumaine," in contrast, unless audiences had exercised heroic self-discipline in thought control, would have suggested du Maine or de Mayenne, brother of the Guise, and Navarre's formidable opponent. Then in July

[19] H. B. Charlton, "The Date of *Love's Labour's Lost*," *Modern Language Review*, 13 (1918), 17.

1593 Navarre mightily offended Elizabeth and her nation by turning his religious coat and buying Paris "for a mass." It has been argued that such events made Shakespeare's character names "topical."[20] Rather they made the names a-topical or contra-topical. The author had been unlucky in his choice. Tucker Brooke has put the matter best: "Doubtless Shakespeare first devised his fiction of Navarre and France at a period when it was possible to weave into it recent names and incidents [i.e. involving French embassies to Navarre in 1578–1586] still too vague in their connotation for English auditors to jar against the playful spirit of the comedy ... [but] to say nothing (virtually) of the military fame of the four gentlemen and associate Dumaine in friendship with the rest, or alternatively to confuse Dumaine with d'Aumont, would have affronted common intelligence if attempted very long after the death of Henry III (Aug. 2, 1589) had brought them all upon the centre of the political stage."[21] It is hard to believe that *Love's Labor's Lost* could have been written or even performed in England between August 1589 and July 1593, or that its character names would have been voluntarily chosen between 1593 and 1598. Toward the end of the latter period they could have been tolerated in a revival. They were worked into the metrical pattern of a number of lines and would have been hard to excise. Besides, luck was running again with the author. After 1595 Navarre somewhat rehabilitated his name by making war on Spain and aligning himself again with the English. He and du Maine ceased to be enemies. But there would still have been small motive for associating four such portentous names in scenes of pastoral jollity even in 1596–1598—and in referring only to a "war" in which Navarre

[20] Ibid. Of course, it can by no means be assumed that H. B. Charlton still holds to views expressed in an article back in the times of the First World War.

[21] The Yale Shakespeare edition (1925), pp. 129, 134.

had assisted the "King of France" and incurred certain expenses.

Some of those who have dated the original version of the play in the midnineties have been a little discomfited by the facts just reviewed. Dover Wilson admits the curious fact that in Shakespeare's play there is not the "slightest reference" to the war, and surmises that "in 1593 Shakespeare had worked over the manuscript of a 'French comedy' dealing with the incidents referred to [i.e. those of the 1578 French embassy to Navarre] and originally plotted by another dramatist somewhere in the 'eighties."[22] This does not make quite clear whether the "French comedy" envisioned was a comedy in French or a comedy about France. If the first is intended, I know of no school of French drama of the time which discussed the affairs of the contemporary *haute monde,* using the names of actual lords. If the second is intended, I see no reason why it should have been "originally plotted by another dramatist" rather than Shakespeare himself. In any case "somewhere in the 'eighties" is something of a concession.

An elusive "French comedy" reappears in some curious remarks by W. W. Greg: "Such adumbration of contemporary characters, particularly in an amiable light, is not exactly what we should expect after Henri IV had forfeited English sympathy by turning Catholic in the summer of 1593, and there are references in the play that point to a date later than this. It is possible, therefore, that Shakespeare worked on the basis of an earlier 'French comedy' that drew upon sources not generally available; but even if that was the case, there is no necessity to suppose that he took from it more than the general situation together with a few names and incidental allusions."[23] The phrase "not exactly what we should expect" strikes me as an understatement, and unless there are inferences in the

[22] New Cambridge edition, pp. 128, 130.
[23] *The Shakespeare First Folio,* p. 219.

passage that escape me, its end contradicts its beginning. Shakespeare, using a "French comedy," voluntarily selected from it those very names the involuntary selection of which the French comedy was originally hypothesized to explain. It seems to me simpler to suppose that he wrote his play about 1588–1589 when the selection of the names was logical, and revised it about 1596–1597 when the retention of the names were permissible.

My final question is, why should a play written for adult professionals in the midnineties so much resemble plays written for child professionals in the mideighties? The resemblance is not superficial. It is observable in content, form, and spirit. It seems highly suggestive that all the basic ingredients of the play became available in a cluster in the decade before 1588, and nothing that became available thereafter was used except incidental phrases. Although I agree with many students of the play that the Holofernes-Nathaniel dialogues belong to the revision, my present point does not hinge upon this assumption.

This is no place to discuss in detail the "sources" of *Love's Labor's Lost*. Its central situation bears some relation to an actual visit in 1578 to Henry of Navarre at Nérac by Marguerite de Valois and her mother, Catherine of France. The royal visitors were accompanied by *l'escadron volant* of ladies in waiting, and Aquitaine was discussed as part of Marguerite's dowry. (The parallels with Shakespeare's play were first noted in a good article by John Phelps in 1899[24] and not,

---

[24] "The Source of Love's Labour's Lost," *Shakespeare Association Bulletin*, 17 (1942), 97–102. (This reprints from the *Baltimore Sun* the article of 1899; the author generously assumes that later publications represent independent discovery.) Other embassies to the court of Navarre have been mentioned as supplying suggestion, but none after 1586. See Geoffrey Bullough, *Narrative and Dramatic Sources of Shakespeare*, I (London, 1957), 425–442.

as invariably stated, in a bad book by Abel Lefranc in 1919.) The negotiations were of a kind to provoke continental gossip, which seems to have reached the ears of Shakespeare, but they were not epoch-making, and the interest in the gossip would not long have survived the more spectacular relations between France and Navarre of 1589 and later. By 1595 such gossip would have been very "old hat." The idea of a Gallic contemplative retreat (associated with Anjou rather than Navarre) appears in de la Primaudaye's *French Academy,* translated into English in 1586. The stock characters of commedia dell'arte, which seem to have influenced the conception of Armado and Moth, not to speak of Holofernes and Nathaniel, became known to the English through the visits of Italian troupes to London before 1588.[25] The plays of Lyly whose specific influence is discernible in *Love's Labor's Lost* were written between 1584 and 1588. Lyly enthusiasts may have overstated the indebtedness, but it remains true that in *Campaspe* there is an incipient philosophical "academy" and a conflict between love and kingly resolves. (In fact the claim of military austerity, or of friendship, or of philosophical detachment as opposed to the claim of love between the sexes was a staple theme of the early "courtesy books" as well as of the chorister drama for genteel audiences.) In *Gallathea* (III.i) Diana's nymphs successively confess their broken vows and agree collectively to succumb to passion; there is certainly some influence here upon the progressive revelations of recusancy in the most famous scene (IV.iii) in

---

[25] O. J. Campbell, "*Love's Labour's Lost* Restudied," in *Studies in Shakespeare, Milton and Donne. By members of the English Department of the University of Michigan* (Ann Arbor, 1925). Professor Campbell's most telling points are that in the case of the *Capitano,* as Armado, the braggart is less a military swaggerer than a *précieux;* and that in the commedia dell'arte the *Affamato* (parasite) is attached to the *Dottore* (pedant) just as in *Love's Labor's Lost* Nathaniel is attached to Holofernes.

Love's Labor's Lost. In *Endymion* the Sir Tophas-Epiton-Bagoa triad shows more than an accidental resemblance to the Armado-Moth-Jacquenetta triad in *Love's Labor's Lost.* It would be phenomenal if so many reminiscences of Lyly in Shakespeare were a delayed manifestation of 1595. And, finally, the one plot ingredient that has been supposed conclusively to indicate a late date[26] indicates nothing of the kind. The Gray's Inn revels of 1594, in which there was a *conjunction* of Muscovite maskers and blackamoor torch-bearers, has been strongly urged as a source of Shakespeare's play. But there was just this conjunction in an actual court masque of 1510, and, more important, this masque was described in one of Shakespeare's favorite books, *Holinshed's Chronicles,* 1587.[27] Combined with the actual visit of ludicrous Russians to Elizabeth's court in 1583, this would have been suggestion enough; and although the Gray's Inn revelers may have hit upon the device independently, they may also have remembered it in *Love's Labor's Lost:* they are as likely to have been Shakespeare's debtors as his creditors.

The structure of *Love's Labor's Lost* is radically different from that of typical Shakespearean comedy, and the difference is in the direction of Chapel and Paul's drama of the eighties —in the grouping and balancing of characters, the at-least-perfunctory deference to the "unities," the fairly equitable distribution of lines among the characters, the emphasis upon words at the expense of action, the use of scenes as set pieces rather than as links in an integrated plot. One must note also the large number of parts calling for nonadult actors (five women and a boy), and the absence of a professional court jester even in a comic court. So far as the spirit of the piece

[26] Rupert Taylor, *The Date of Love's Labour's Lost,* lays great emphasis on this "source."

[27] Fred Sorenssen, "The Masque of Muscovites in *Love's Labour's Lost,*" *Modern Language Notes,* 50 (1935), 499–501.

is concerned, one hesitates to be frank in the teeth of all that has been said about its adult suavity. It has been praised as representing the vary acme of courtly grace, genteel manners, and sophisticated wit, but a reasonably objective reading, with attention to what the characters are actually saying, somewhat shakes one's faith. It is all in good fun, true enough, but the manners projected are atrocious and the characters uniformly barbarous. Their repartee consists largely in attacks upon each other's morals, intelligence, and personal appearance. When not reviling each other, they are reviling each other's sweethearts, whose complexions suggest to the speakers pockiness, dirt, shoe leather, and other unsavory similes. Some of the retorts are brutal, and they by no means "abrogate scurrility." The one character whose manners achieve a minimal level of social decency is none other than the main butt of the piece—gentle Don Armado. The comic effect derives in the main from impudence, pertness, and animal spirits. In their offstage moments the "king" and his lords are visualized as tumbling about like frolicsome kids.[28] The atmosphere of boisterous juvenility is not a characteristic shared with the plays of Lyly, which are usually quite decorous, but it appears in chorister drama of a later period. I find it more congenial to imagine Love's Labor's Lost originally in the repertory of boy actors rather than of grown men.

That the play may have been written for children has been several times suggested, but there has been a singular reluctance to follow the idea home to its logical conclusion. A play originally written for boys would, we should suppose, originally have been produced by a chorister company in a "private" theatre if such a theatre were operating at the time when the play was written. But even those who have

---

[28] See the interesting passage, v.ii.90–118.

vigorously urged 1588–1589 as the date of original composition, for instance F. G. Fleay and latterly T. W. Baldwin, have stopped short of such a suggestion.[29] Although Professor Baldwin claims too much for the idea of its only-rudimentary adherence to the alleged "five-act structure" as an indication of early date, and concedes too little about the late style and verbal allusions in parts of the play, nevertheless his defense of his dating is often cogent.[30] The trouble is that, like Fleay, he claims the play for Strange's Men playing at the Cross Keys, and it is hard to think of *Love's Labor's Lost* in any form being produced at a converted inn as a rival attraction with a performing horse. None of the popular plays of the eighties resemble it in the least. A decade later, revised, somewhat humanized, and equipped with the sure-fire Holofernes and Nathaniel, it might have gone over as a novelty with a popular audience. Shakespeare himself had helped to educate such audiences in word play: "We must speak by the card, or equivocation will undo us. By the Lord, Horatio, this three years I have taken note of it, the age is grown so picked that the toe of the peasant comes so near the heel of the courtier he galls his kibe." Still, we must remember that the play is never listed with his popular hits in its own time, and the only specifically indicated performances are those before Queen Elizabeth and Queen Anne.[31]

[29] See Campbell, "*Love's Labour's Lost* Restudied," p. 11; David, New Arden edition, p. l. Charles Knight in the introductory notice to the play in his *Pictorial Edition of the Works of Shakespeare* (London, 1839–1843) proposes that the play was written in 1589 when Shakespeare "was a joint-proprietor in the Blackfriars theatre" (I, 76), but he seems, unfortunately, to have confused the second Blackfriars, acquired by the King's Men ca. 1608, with the first Blackfriars, closed as a theatre in 1584.

[30] *Shakespeare's Five-Act Structure* (Urbana, Ill., 1947), p. 635.

[31] The second quarto, 1631, reprinting the play from the first folio "As it was acted by his Maiesties Seruants at the Blacke-Friers and the Globe" suggests a Caroline revival.

In 1588–1589 there were facilities for such a play as *Love's Labor's Lost* in the commercial theatre of London. Although the Chapel Children had lost the first Blackfriars in 1584, they retained at least a shadowy existence. We hear of them on tour at Norwich in 1586–1587 and at Leicester in 1590–1591.[32] In 1594 two plays were published with identical inscriptions, "Played by the children of her Maiesties Chappell."[33] Although both seem considerably earlier than the year of publication, both contain writing later than 1584 when the Blackfriars ceased operating. However, the Paul's theatre provides the more interesting possibility. This remained open until 1590, generating plays which were good enough for occasional selection for performance at court. All we have of what must have been an extensive repertory is a few plays by John Lyly. We know positively that there were other plays and other playwrights. Let me propose that Shakespeare's *Love's Labor's Lost* in its original form was written for Paul's in 1588–1589 and see what the hypothesis suggests.

The abruptness with which unmistakable allusions to Shakespeare in London begin to appear in 1590–1593 creates the impression that his presence there, as distinct from the allusions, was also abrupt. Chambers seems to predicate a swift translation from Stratford to London in 1590, and an equally swift transformation of a provincial artisan or idler of twenty-six into an actor and playwright. In view of the general paucity of allusions to particular companies, plays, and playwrights in and before the period in question, the evidence will bear no such construction, and the probabilities are against it. Neither, in view of the circumstances, does the allusion to him as an "upstart crow" mean that he was *really* an upstart; and we know definitely that the work he himself called the "first heir" of his invention was not *really* the first.

---

[32] J. T. Murray, *English Dramatic Companies* (London, 1910), I, 337.
[33] *The Wars of Cyrus,* and Marlowe and Nashe's *Tragedy of Dido.*

Those who predicate for him an earlier career in the theatre try to trace back the ancestry of the Chamberlain's and Strange's companies and then postulate his association with such shadowy combinations of actors as emerge. This is better, but also vulnerable, since there was always much recruiting as well as realignment among acting groups. We do not know how Shakespeare became an actor: he may have joined a country troupe after he reached his majority; he may have come to London and haunted the theatres; he may have become a chapel boy in the household of a lord and been superannuated into the theatre. In 1582 Stephen Gosson speaks of actors "trained up from their childhood in this abominable exercise,"[34] and there is no lack of later evidence of chapel actors graduating into adult companies. As Hamlet says of the little eyases, "Will they not say afterwards if they should grow themselves to common players (as it is most like, if their means are no better), their writers do them wrong to make them exclaim against their own succession?" That Shakespeare himself may have walked this route has long been recognized as possible. We know that he was born in 1564, that he married and became a father in 1582–1583, and that his wife bore him twins in Stratford in 1585. But marrying and even begetting twins are not exclusive occupations. His residence in Stratford from childhood may have been intermittent, and he may have been selected as a chapel child, as the gifted sons of plain people frequently were. It is not only the period between his production of twin children in Stratford in 1585 and his production of twin plays in London in 1590–1591 that must be designated the "lost years."

As a chapel child, dwelling part of the time in a great house, part of the time behind his father's shop, Shakespeare

[34] *Plays Confuted in Five Actions* (1582), in *English Drama and Stage,* ed. W. C. Hazlitt (London, 1869), p. 215.

would have gained that insight into two worlds which is one of his most striking characteristics. He would have continued with the education in Latin begun in the Stratford grammar school. As a youth he might have taught younger chapel boys, and guided them in the performance of plays. I wish now to bring together some scattered data which have never been satisfactorily explained and which may have some bearing on our subject. The solitary item in the "Shakespeare mythos" which scholars have been inclined to take seriously is John Aubrey's jotting, "He understood Latin pretty well: for he had been in his younger years a School-master in the Countrey."[35] There are several reasons for taking it seriously: the information came from Beeston, the son of a member of Shakespeare's own acting company; there is nothing scandalous about it such as would have appealed to Aubrey; there is nothing "generic" about it like the stories of deer poaching and the like; and finally there is nothing in the least striking or colorful about it such as would suggest any reason for communicating it except the fact that it was true.

Now what does "School-master in the Countrey" suggest? To the American it suggests "country schoolmaster," perhaps evoking an image of Ichabod Crane. To the English I suspect that it suggests Nickleby's term of servitude in Dotheboys Hall, and perhaps the reference to the "charge-house on the top of the mountain" (v.i. 72) where Holofernes presides would fortify this impression. I am ignorant of the various routes to the teaching profession in the sixteenth century, but I am inclined to believe that a regular "schoolmaster" would normally be a university graduate, and that the equivalent of an usher would only be found in a sizable school in a sizable town. My guess is that "in the Countrey" as Beeston or Aubrey would use the term would mean "in a country

---

[35] Chambers, *William Shakespeare*, II, 254.

house"—the seat of a landed gentleman or nobleman. Here a nonuniversity youth might quite well pass on such Latin as he had acquired to the more youthful recruits of the chapel, taking this load off the chaplain.

Chapels in the environs of London transformed themselves into regular acting companies, the occupants of "private" theatres. Chapels "in the country" sometimes went on theatrical tours. The "Earl of Oxford's Company" played at Bristol in 1581, "being I man and IX boys."[36] In 1581 Shakespeare was seventeen, "a codling when 'tis almost an apple: 'tis with him in standing water, between man and boy"; hence we might cast him either as the "I man" or one of the "IX boys" and remember that an association with Oxford's chapel could have landed him in 1584 squarely in the first Blackfriars theatre—as a coach and writer, of course, rather than as a juvenile actor. We may write off Oxford entirely (baleful name in Shakespearean speculation) and still recognize that Shakespeare may have penetrated the acting profession by almost growing up in it. We must always recognize that such an unusual man must have been an unusual boy and youth, and that there were "divers of worship" other than Oxford who could have brought him into the orbit of the Blackfriars and Paul's theatricals. With F. P. Wilson I fully agree that he must have known he was a poet from the first. I should go further and say that anyone who wrote plays like his of the early nineties, inferior though they may be when compared to his own later work, had nevertheless been writing plays for a considerable length of time.

Shakespeare lacked the family connections and the university degree of a John Lyly, such as might have put him in charge of a chapel company, but he could have served as a "Johannes factotum." Chapel masters had at one time acted

---

[36] Murray, *English Dramatic Companies*, I, 345.

with their boys, and occasional roles in the plays of Lyly, such as that of Sir Tophas, suggest that the tradition of including an adult actor may have been maintained. Perhaps an adult who had been a chapel-boy actor would have been a useful adjunct about Paul's when long commercialization had rendered acting *infra dig* for the chapel master or the genteel entrepreneur associated with him. A good adult voice may have been useful too—and a good composer of songs. This brings me to a second of the unsolved puzzles about the drama of the time. Who wrote the songs for Lyly's plays, nearly all of which were excluded from editions during Lyly's lifetime? W. W. Greg's argument that Lyly did not write them is better than his argument that Dekker did.[37] Some of them are not only worthy of Shakespeare, but are as much in his vein as in Dekker's, notably Appeles' song and Trico's song (v.i) in *Campaspe*. The latter reminds us of the concluding songs in *Love's Labor's Lost,* and contains phrases either repeated in or plagiarized from Shakespeare's own "Hark, hark, the lark."

The final unsolved puzzle I wish to mention is one of the strangest in our early dramatic history. Who was the subject of Spenser's lines in the lament of Thalia in *The Teares of the Muses,* registered in 1590 and printed in 1591 in *Complaints?*

> And he the man, whom Nature selfe had made
> To mock her selfe, and Truth to imitate,
> With kindly counter vnder Mimick shade,
> Our pleasant *Willy,* ah is dead of late:
> With whom all ioy all iolly meriment
> Is also deaded, and in dolour drent.

[37] "On the Authorship of the Songs in Lyly's Plays," *Modern Language Review,* 1 (1905), 43–52. What appears to be a debased version of Trico's song printed in Dekker's *Sun's Darling* in 1656 is taken by Greg to be the "original" version of the song printed in Lyly's *Six Court Comedies* in 1632; I cannot follow the reasoning.

In stead therof scoffing Scurrilitie,
And scornfull Follie with Contempt is crept,
Rolling in rymes of shameles ribaudrie
Without regard, or due Decorum kept,
Each idle wit at will presumes to make,
And doth the Learneds task vpon him take.

But that same gentle Spirit, from whose pen
Large streames of honnie and sweete Nectar flowe,
Scorning the boldnes of such base-borne men,
Which dare their follies forth so rashlie throwe;
Doth rather chooose to sit in idle Cell,
Than so himself to mockerie to sell.[38]

If Shakespeare suddenly appeared in the role of playwright in 1590, of course the lines could not refer to him. If he had been writing long enough for an interval to have occurred in his output just before 1590, the case is quite different. It is easy to say that Shakespeare was not the subject of the lines, but it is almost as easy to say that *no one* was the subject of the lines; it is impossible to name anyone writing joyous poetic comedy before 1590 with talent enough to command Spenser's respect. But there the lines stand, demanding an explanation; such comedies must have been written, or Thalia would have had nothing to lament. After canvassing the field, Chambers happily rejects his own suggestion of Dick Tarlton, then, in fault of better, hits upon John Lyly. But the lines do not suggest the literary personality of John Lyly, and Lyly was not

---

[38] Chambers, *William Shakespeare*, II, 186–187. Chambers also rejects as a reference to Shakespeare Spenser's lines in *Colin Clout's Come Home Again* (1592–1595): "And there though last not least is *Aetion,* / A gentler shepheard may no where be found: / Whose *Muse* full of high thoughts inuention, / Doth like himselfe Heroically sound." The last line suggests the heroic-sounding name "Shakespeare," and although Lee's ready acceptance of the identification seems a little uncritical, Chambers' ready rejection seems a little captious; the possibility remains open.

inactive as a playwright in 1589–1590; in fact he was involved in the Marprelate controversy; and it was the "scoffing Scurrilitie" and "shameles ribaudrie" of the plays of this controversy which led to the closing of Paul's and presumably to Thalia's lament. It is easy enough to guess what spate of comedies Spenser deplored; the difficulty lies in guessing what kindly comedies preceded them.

I am led to two reflections: first, that if anyone in his times was equipped to recognize Shakespeare's talents promptly, and to recognize their essential quality, it was Edmund Spenser; and second, that if Spenser's lines really did refer to Shakespeare, it would be the irony of the ages that the fact remains unconceded. After detecting allusions to Shakespeare in every likely and unlikely place, we would have failed to detect one in "our pleasant Willy . . . that same gentle Spirit." The idea of Shakespeare as the source of "streams of honnie and sweet Nectar" furnishes the first critical cliché that appears in authenicated allusions to his writing; and the idea of Shakespeare as one "whom Nature selfe had made To mock herself, and Truth to imitate" (i.e. that he was as true to nature as nature herself) furnishes the second critical cliché and the one which endured for a century and a half. Perhaps it is just too obvious to be believed.

No one in his right mind would wish to associate Shakespeare with the coterie theatres rather than the popular theatres, which produced the best drama of the era and where he obviously realized himself. But an apprenticeship in the coterie theatres would not have been disabling; players destined for the big leagues often begin in the little leagues. No one, either, would wish to part scholarly company with such men as E. K. Chambers, G. L. Kittredge, W. W. Greg, and F. P. Wilson in order to link arms with Furnivall and Fleay. Our twentieth-century "paragons of caution" have performed a great service in resisting "disintegration," super-subtle theo

ries about ur-texts, progressive revision and the like. They
have assumed, reasonably, that the existing texts of plays
are the "original" texts or at least the ones most worth dating
and discussing. But occasionally these scholars, useful though
their stalwart skepticism has been, may have overstated their
cases; and in their anxiety to shore up the wind-racked structure of Shakespearean scholarship, they may have boarded up
certain doors.

I have proved nothing in this article, but I hope I have
indicated why I should be sorry if the opinion that *Love's
Labor's Lost* was first written in the midnineties should in-
exorably "harden into an orthodoxy." I think that this play
is more likely than any other to suggest the avenues of investigation if there is ever to be a "breakthrough" in our
knowledge of Shakespeare's theatrical beginnings. If I may
resort once more to the jargon of our technological age, it is
the only play, with the possible exception of *The Comedy of
Errors*,[39] which contains "built-in" evidence of a date before
1590, along with hints of the original auspices of production.

[39] I think the two plays should be studied in tandem. *The Comedy of
Errors* may have originally been chorister-company Plautine "contamina-
tion" with intrigues multiplied in the fashion of Lyly's *Mother Bombie*,
then later supplied with its humanizing frame. W. W. Greg observes that
some of the stage directions suggest "a set stage with three houses" (*The
Shakespeare First Folio*, p. 200). Such suggestion of a localized or scenic
stage is a characteristic of all eleven texts of chorister drama before 1590,
and *Love's Labor's Lost* itself could have been set "in pastoral" as could
some of the plays of Lyly. The allusion in *The Comedy of Errors* to France
"armed and reverted, making war against her heir" (iii.ii.126) may belong
to any time between August 1589 and July 1593, but signifies little if the text
has been revised. A stronger link with *Love's Labor's Lost* is the fact that
both texts share certain peculiarities and seem to have been set up from
the same kind of copy. See Greg, *Shakespeare First Folio*, p. 203n.

The Tragical History, Admirable Atchievments and various events of Guy Earl Of Warwick, A Tragedy Acted very Frequently with great Applause, By his late Majesties Servants. Written by B.J. So reads a title page of 1661. The "B.J." probably means that the publishers, Thomas Vere and William Gilbertson, having a stray theatrical piece to vend, wished to suggest the name which in 1661 and for a few years thereafter headed the roll of honor of past writers for the stage. The "Acted very Frequently . . . By his late Majesties Servants" was certainly invented for promotional purposes. No play so primitive as this *Guy Earl of Warwick* could have been performed by the leading company of London in the reign of Charles I. Even *Mucedorus,* revived by the King's Men early in the reign of James, is sophisticated by comparison.

In his *Dictionary of Old English Plays* Halliwell-Phillipps suggested that the play might be identical with "the life and death of Guy of Warwicke" entered in the Stationers' Register January 15, 1620, as by Day and Dekker—to which A. H. Bullen responded, "I doubt whether either of the authors, if they had tried, could have written so execrably."[1] The remark seems (understandably) to have abated the zeal of investigators, but the piece is not really contemptible. It conveys an impression of ineptitude because its type had become archaic at the time of its publication, or even of the registration of the Day and Dekker title. Bullen would have spoken more tolerantly if he had associated it with that earlier period of

Adapted from "An Early Attack upon Shakespeare?," *Shakespeare Association Bulletin,* vol. 16 (1941).

[1] *Works of John Day* (London, 1881), p. 11.

the drama when Christian piety and the cardinal virtues were still addressing audiences from the lips of peripatetic knights. Either it was already old in 1620 or its author was quite clever in faking antiques. The lines,

> His sacred fury menaceth that Nation,
> Which hath Indea under Sequestration.
> He doth not strike at Surplices and Tippits
> (To bring an Oleo in of Sects in Sippits),

suggest the sixteenth rather than the seventeenth century, even though the topical allusions are the most "modern" in the play.

The *Guy Earl of Warwick* of 1661, is, I believe, a composition of ca. 1592–1593, cut for itinerant performance but otherwise little altered. We can safely postulate the appearance of a Guy of Warwick play early in the nineties. Henslowe records performances of a *Huon of Bordeux* in 1593 and of a *Godfrey of Boulogne* (part two) in 1594,[2] and although we must not create "facts" for our convenience, it is hard to believe that the English hero would have been passed over when Londoners were being offered the foreign worthies with whom he was so closely associated. One episode in the play (featuring "Oberon") derives from the Huon of Bordeaux legend, and most of the other details from the metrical romance of Guy which had been available in various editions since the end of the fifteenth century.[3] It was uninfluenced by later accretions to the legend, for instance those in Samuel Rowlands' narrative poem *The Famous History of Guy Earl of Warwicke*, 1608, which succeeded to the popularity form-

---

[2] *Henslowe's Diary*, ed. W. W. Greg, pt. I (London, 1904), pp. 16, 18. The "2 pte of godfrey of bullen" is specified as new. The first part, like our hypothesized Warwick play, missed recording in the *Diary*.

[3] R. S. Crane, "The Vogue of Guy of Warwick," *PMLA*, 30 (1915), 164–165.

erly enjoyed by the metrical romance. The latest "source" that has been suggested for the play, *A Plesante songe of the valiant actes of Guy of Warwick*, was printed in 1592. As in the case of other broadside ballads, it was perhaps not a source but a spin-off of the play itself as first performed.

The best indication of an early date is the play itself. It is constructed like the early biographical chronicles, such as Marlowe's *Doctor Faustus*, with the exploits of the hero regularly coupled with the drolleries of the hero's clownish servant, while a Chorus or Presenter (in this case "Time") narrates deeds not presented in the action. The following exchange, from the considerable portion of the dialogue in rhyme, gives an idea of the general quaintness:

> *Phillis.* Give me some Bread, I prethee Father Eat.
> *Guy.* Give me Brown Bread, for thats a Pilgrimes Meat.
> *Phillis.* Reach me some Wine, good Father tast of this.
> *Guy.* Give me cold Water that my Comfort is. . . . (act v)

Time's prologue provides a fair sampling of the blank verse:

> Renowned Sir Guy of Warwick whose great Name,
> makes England famous in all after times,
> for nursing up so brave a Martiallist.
> Time now renues his fortunes to the world
> and layes them open to your Gentle Views;
> think then with apprehensive eyes you see
> this warlike Lord boldly attempt to fight,
> with that fell savage Bore of Calledon
> that spoiles the fields and murders passengers,
> him hath his sword subdu'd . . . .
> . . . . imagine then,
> King Athelstone hath left fair Winchester
> and here in Warwick Castle keeps his Court.
> What follows now of Guy and his fair Deeds,
> sit and behold, the story now proceeds.

The use of a choral spokesman to abridge the action was a device still available in the year of Shakespeare's *Henry the Fifth,* but another play of that year contains an apology; the muse, at the beginning of Dekker's *Old Fortunatus,*

> ... begs your pardon, for sheele send me foorth,
> Not when the lawes of Poesy doe call,
> But as the storie needes.

The device was already old-fashioned in 1599. The second choral speech in *Old Fortunatus* and the third in *Guy Earl of Warwick* both end in a touch of whimsy:

> Suppose you see him [Fortunatus] brought to Babylon;
> And that the Sunne (clothed all in fire) hath rid
> One quarter of his hot celestiall way
> With the bright morning, and that in this instant,
> He and the Soldan meete, but what they say
> Listen you, the talke of kings none dare bewray.

Compare:

> long stories are not told in little time,
> much matter in small room we must combyne. . . .
> if it be long, say length is all the fault,
> if it be lame, say old men needs must halt.

One could scarcely claim here a "parallel," but Dekker cannot be summarily dismissed as the possible author of *Guy Earl of Warwick.*

It is by no means improbable that Dekker's playmaking career began as early as 1592–1593. The pace at which he was writing in 1598, when Henslowe began recording the names of authors in his diary, argues that he was already an old hand and the probable author of some of the anonymous plays listed by Henslowe in earlier years. Since he acted as reviser of his own *Phaeton* and *Old Fortunatus,* we might infer

that he was the author of *Tasso's Melancholy*, 1594, revised by
him in 1602. A Henslowe play of 1595 was called *Disguises*,
and a play of this title is listed as Dekker's in Hill's catalogue
of manuscripts.[4] In 1592–1593 Dekker was just approaching
his majority, and he could surely have written the following
lines without trying to write "execrably":

Thus Time concludes this dolent History,
And ends this Scene with Guy of Warwick's death;
So what is it but Time can bring to passe?
Time layes up Treasure where ther's Vertue scant,
And gives the silly Fool when wise Men want;
Both Poor and Rich confesse my power Divine,
And every one doth say, make much of Time,
Through the whole World, while the World was, Time rangeth,
And 'tis mens manners and not Time that changeth.
Of you whose souls look for Eternity,
Rest in the peace of perpetuity,
And kindly grant to this request of mine;
For he's but young that writes of this Old Time.
Therefore if this your eyes or ears may please,
He means to show you better things than these.

Dekker in his prime often indulged in this kind of plain-
man's philosophizing (to the disgust of the more austere of
modern critics), and there are lines in *Guy Earl of Warwick*
which might have appeared in any of his plays:

The longest Summers day comes to an end,
the dial points though none perceive it stur. (act v)

those that have learned of Angells how to sing
and to the world all piety doth bring
and fill the world with learning and with art,
to those doth Time her Golden gifts impart. (act iii)

[4] J. Q. Adams, "Hill's List of Plays in Manuscript," *Library*, N.S., vol.
20 (1939).

The weighers of "internal evidence" such as Fleay and Sykes have come into somewhat ill repute, and it is true that their methods rarely deserved the confidence they so contentiously displayed, but they did in fact read closely and their findings can not be discarded *in toto*. Sykes[5] has noted Dekker's fondness for iteration, and we may observe in *Guy Earl of Warwick:* "O Master, the Devil, the Devil, the Devil" (act II); "Tarry, tarry, tarry, hold, hold, hold" (act III); "O my belly, my belly, my belly" (act V). He has noted that "Hellhound" is one of Dekker's most distinctive terms of abuse, and we observe in the present play, "Hell-hound come forth, that I may cope with thee" (act II). Some other details may be significant. Oberon awakens Guy of Warwick with music:

Nymphes, Satyres, Fawnes, and all the fairy train,
that waits on Oberon the fairy King,
attend me quickly with your silver tunes:
and in a circled ring, lets compass round,
this sleeping Knight that lies upon the ground.
      [Enter the Fairies with Musick....]
Guy. Where art thou Guy? what heavenly place is this? (act II)

When Dekker's Fortune awakens Old Fortunatus with music, his response is identical,

   Oh, how am I transported? Is this earth?
   Or blessed Elizium? (I, i)

And in view of Oberon's "silver tunes" we may notice Dekker's association of silver and music:

   I tride and found it true: and secretly
   Commaunded Musicke with her silver tongue,
   To chime soft lullabies into his soul....
      (*Old Fortunatus*, II, i)

[5] H. D. Sykes, *Sidelights on Elizabethan Drama* (London, 1924), p. 106.

> Musicke talke lowder, that thy siluer voice
> May reach my Soueraignes eares.
>
> *(Satiromastix*, ii, i)

I offer one more parallel, perhaps the most impressive. The familiar line in the song of the basket-makers in *Patient Grissel,*

> Canst drink the water of the Crisped spring,
> O sweet content!

perfects a distich in the last act of *Guy Earl of Warwick,*

> ... Your great lord and I
> have thought our selves as happy as a King
> to drink the water of a Christal spring. (act v)

(I assume that Dekker's claim to the song is still recognized as good.)

Such evidence might be dismissed as trivial were it not for the Stationers' Register entry of 1620 actually associating Dekker with a Guy of Warwick play. He and Day may well have reworked a piece written by Dekker at the beginning of his career. That plays of the nineties were reworked for the new generation must be accepted as a general proposition: even the skeptical Sir Walter Greg[6] was inclined to accept Fleay's suggestion that Dekker and Massinger's *Virgin Martyr,* acted at the Red Bull in 1620, was a new version of *Diocletian* mentioned by Henslowe in 1594. In this instance we assume that we have an extant revision of a lost original. In the Guy of Warwick instance we must assume that we have the extant original of a lost revision.

The extant *Guy Earl of Warwick* can be imagined as pleasing London audiences in the early nineties and country audiences long thereafter. On October 14, 1618, John Taylor the water poet was stopping at the Maidenhead Inn, Islington,

---

[6] *Henslowe's Diary,* ed. W. W. Greg, pt. II (London, 1908), p. 172.

where "we had a play of the Life and Death of Guy of Warwick, played by the Right Honourable the Earl of Derby
his men."[7] The provincial career of these men dated from the
time of the upheaval in the London theatrical world in 1592–
1594. The "Life and Death . . ." in the title of the Guy of Warwick play seen by Taylor and in the title listed in the Stationers' Register might suggest that it was for Derby's Men
that Dekker and Day had collaborated, but it is unlikely that
in 1618–1620 this fringe company would have been employing
these or any other writers.[8] It is more likely that a few of the
old standbys in the repertory of the company survived its
dissolution. In 1632 Thomas Nabbes' *Covent Garden* contains
an allusion to tattered strollers:

> *Ralph.* . . . we shall then be neere the Cockpit,
>   and see a play now and then.
> *Dobs.* But tell me Ralph, are those players the
>   ragged fellowes that were at our house last
>   Christmas, that borrowed the red blanket off
>   my bed to make their Major a gowne; and had
>   the great pot-lid for Guy of Warwicks Buckler?
> *Ralph.* No, Dobson; they are men of credit. (1, i)

Perhaps Vere and Gilbertson should have said of their play,
not that it was acted by "his late Majesties Servants," but that
it was still acted (with bulldog persistence) in "his late
Majesties Reign."

Let me now dismiss all theories about *Guy Earl of Warwick*

[7] *Penniless Pilgrimage,* 1618, in *Old Book Collector's Miscellany,* ed. C.
Hindley, vol. II (1872), no. 10, p. 67.

[8] Since Day as well as Dekker was writing in the nineties, it is possible
that the Stationers' Register record of 1620 represents a belated entry of an
old play, obtained from Derby's Men, 1618–1620, and then passed from
stationer to stationer until 1661. However it is unlikely that Day and
Dekker collaborated very early, certain that they did later: their lost
Bellman of London was licensed for the Prince's Men in 1623.

printed in 1661 except that it is old—as old as 1592–1593. This I firmly believe. Let me also try to reward the reader who has plodded thus far in the hope of hearing something about the "Sparrow of Stratford" named in my inveigling title. Sparrow is the name of the clown whom, in the idiotic fashion of the knightly heroes of the old plays, the Earl of Warwick has chosen as his squire. Sparrow's stupidity and turpitude stand in comic contrast with the Earl's saintliness throughout the latter's passage from youth to old age. Toward the end he encounters his master's son Rainborne, and the following exchange occurs:

> *Rainborne.* ... prethee where wer't born?
> *Sparrow.* I faith Sir I was born in England at Strat-
> ford upon Aven in Warwickshire.
> *Rainborne.* Wer't born in England? What's thy name?
> *Sparrow.* Nay I have a fine finical name, I can tell
> ye, for my name is Sparrow; yet I am no
> house Sparrow, nor no hedge Sparrow, nor no
> peaking Sparrow, nor no sneaking Sparrow,
> but I am a high mounting lofty minded
> Sparrow, and that Parnell knows well enough,
> and a good many more of the pretty Wenches
> of our Parish ifaith. (act v)

Now the servant of a Warwickshire Earl might quite innocently be described as coming from Stratford, but there is something suspicious about this curiously specific information in view of what immediately follows. "Sparrow" was a cant term for a lecher. By no stretch of the imagination could it be described as "a fine finical name." On the other hand "Shakespeare" (which to the incorrigibly suggestible Elizabethans might itself provoke ribald jests) would certainly seem a "fine finical name" to writers so plainly dubbed as "Green" or "Peele"—or the youthful "Dekker." Since the latter became Green's literary disciple, he can easily be imagined as Green's partisan. At no point in the play has Sparrow revealed Shakespearean traits (other than an addiction to bad puns), but unless he had a prototype who supposed himself "as well able to bombast out a blank verse with the best," why should he suddenly describe himself as "a high mounting lofty minded Sparrow"? In the literal context of the role "high mounting" is a predictable double entendre, but "lofty minded" seems mysteriously gratuitous.

The passage may be a glancing hit at Shakespeare, written when his mounting star was vexing new writers as well as old. On the other hand it may not. Of one thing we may be certain: if *Guy of Warwick* had been published in 1592–1593 instead of misleadingly in 1661, the passage would by now have inspired volumes of commentary. The Sparrow from Stratford, sneak thief of the pagans' "snap-sacks," would vie with the Upstart Crow as a bird of scholarly contention. Sparrow's lordly master would have thrown a flickering light upon a wide range of lordly recipients of the sonnets, while Sparrow's "sweet wench Parnell" would have moved among the shadows of the o'erhastily married Anne, of Willobie his Avisa, and of the dark lady.[9] A host of opportunities have been missed. Perhaps it is not too late—or perhaps it is just as well.

[9] He has got his "precious Parnell" with child before leaving Stratford, and he describes himself as "bird of Venus and a Cock of the game" (act II).

*I*N INTRODUCING the *Mermaid* selection of Ford's plays, Havelock Ellis spoke of *Perkin Warbeck* as free alike of the characteristic merits and defects of the author—"an exception to every generalization that may be arrived at concerning his work" and "the least interesting of his plays for those who care for the peculiar qualities which mark Ford's genius."[1] Some years later T. S. Eliot wrote appreciatively of Ford, but revealed a certain imperviousness to the charm of his "peculiar qualities" by nominating *Perkin Warbeck* as his finest play.[2] Recently this dramatist has been more closely considered than any other of Shakespeare's contemporaries and successors, in scores of articles and in five full-length books;[3] and although the critics have varied in their estimate of *Perkin Warbeck,* they have demurred in general at Eliot's judgment that it is their poet's best, thus proving themselves true Fordians in Havelock Ellis' sense. In the context of this body of criticism, each denial of the superiority of the play attests to its exceptional character.

Although it is easy to illustrate that *Perkin Warbeck* is so different from Ford's other plays as to embarrass his admirers,

From *Studies in the English Renaissance Drama in Memory of Karl Julius Holzknecht,* ed. J. W. Bennett, O. Cargill, and V. Hall, Jr. (New York, New York University Press, 1951).

[1] Havelock Ellis, ed., *John Ford,* the Mermaid Series (London, n.d.), pp. xii–xiii.

[2] T. S. Eliot, "John Ford," *Selected Essays* (London, 1932, 1951).

[3] M. Joan Sargeaunt, *John Ford* (Oxford, 1935); G. F. Sensabaugh, *The Tragic Muse of John Ford* (Stanford, Calif., 1944); Robert Davril, *Le Drame de John Ford* (Paris, 1954); H. F. Oliver, *The Problem of John Ford* (Melbourne, 1955); Clifford Leech, *John Ford and the Drama of His Time* (London, 1957).

its mystery still remains. What induced Ford to stray so far from Ford? I suggest that the solution to this mystery resides in a cognate mystery. In discussing *The Witch of Edmonton,* by Rowley, Dekker, and Ford, Havelock Ellis remarked that "it is one of those plays, not uncommon at that time, in which two or more writers united to produce something that was unlike their individual work, and often superior to anything they produced singly."[4] The phenomenon was less common than the words imply, but it did occur, and we may profitably observe a few instances.

No fact in theatrical history is more firmly established than that *Eastward Hoe* was written by Jonson, Chapman, and Marston. If by some miracle they proved not to have been the authors, then no other fact in theatrical history is more certain than that Dekker and Middleton had nothing to do with the play. It was a kind of rejoinder at Blackfriars to *Westward Hoe* of Paul's, and the latter was written in part by Dekker himself. Furthermore, Dekker and Middleton were collaborating on plays for the Fortune when *Eastward Hoe* appeared. Assuming, however, that we knew none of these things but were examining *Eastward Hoe* as an anonymous play, I believe that we would confidently assign it to Dekker and Middleton, who certainly did not write it, and confidently deny it to Jonson, Marston, and Chapman, who certainly did. It is unlike anything each of the latter wrote singly, and even more unlike anything we can imagine their writing together.

Another instance is provided by *The Knight of the Burning Pestle,* declared by the title page of the quarto of 1635 to be by Beaumont and Fletcher. We eliminate Fletcher on stylistic grounds, fortified by the knowledge that the play differs greatly in tone from anything written by him singly.

---

[4] *John Ford,* p. xiii.

This leaves us with Beaumont, whom we accept as the author, conveniently forgetting that the play differs almost as greatly from anything written by him singly. Among less famous plays, *A Looking Glass for London and England* is quite unlike those written by Lodge and Greene singly, and *Appius and Virginia* is equally unlike those written by Webster and Heywood singly.

Now it is observable that at least three of the four plays cited above were written under conditions that would encourage self-discipline. When *A Looking Glass* was written, its type was already obsolete, and the play was, so to speak, a "reproduction." *Eastward Hoe* was a conscious departure from the usual comic fare at Blackfriars and the vein of its several authors. And of course *The Knight of the Burning Pestle* was a parody. The conditions were right in each case for the momentary suppression of the more individualistic traits of the various writers engaged. To suggest a modern analogy, if Eliot and Housman had been impelled to collaborate upon a poem several decades ago, we cannot conceive of any merit or homogeneity in the result—unless, perchance, the poem were of a type distinct from any they were accustomed to writing individually. Together they might have produced an excellent imitation of a medieval ballad, or an admirable parody of Pope. Similarly, Booth Tarkington and Sinclair Lewis could never have collaborated successfully upon a realistic novel of American life, but they might have produced a very good detective story.

It is commonly recognized that the chronicle play was obsolete when *Perkin Warbeck* was written. It is not so commonly recognized that bourgeois tragedy was just as obsolete when *The Witch of Edmonton* was written. In type it belongs with *Arden of Feversham* and *A Woman Killed with Kindness* rather than with the coeval *Women Beware Women*. A working hypothesis begins to emerge. Both

Perkin Warbeck and *The Witch of Edmonton* are belated examples of dramatic types that had enjoyed their heyday several decades earlier. Both are fine examples of their types. Both are remarkably homogeneous. Both baffle us when we try to relate them to the usual vein of their accepted authors. One of these plays is a collaborative work by Dekker, Rowley, and Ford, created under the conditions noted above as disciplining idiosyncrasy. May not the other, like it in so many respects, be also like it in respect to composite authorship? Let us assume tentatively that *Perkin Warbeck* was written in collaboration by Dekker, Rowley, and Ford. Why has no one detected in the play the presence of so individual a writer as Dekker? This may be answered by another question. Were it not for his name on the title page, encouraging the application of verbal tests, who would have detected in *The Witch of Edmonton* the presence of so individual a writer as Ford? And what about this matter of title pages? Dekker's name is missing from that of *Perkin Warbeck,* but so also is Ford's. The latter's anagram is there as on several others, *fide honor,* and he signed the dedication, beginning "Ovt of the darknesse of a former Age (enlighten'd by a late, both learned, and an honourable pen) I haue endevoured, to personate a great Attempt. . . ." The inference is that Ford wrote the play and wrote it alone, but it remains an inference. If charged with appropriating the work of others, Ford might have said that he had done nothing of the kind —as witness the reticent title page and the allusion to a "late, both learned, and an honourable pen," which we assume to be Francis Bacon's but was intended as Thomas Dekker's. Dekker died in 1632, and the play was published in 1633. Ford, who was legally trained, would have been technically in the clear.

These insinuations of sharp practices are not seriously intended. They are merely a warning that we ourselves must not grow too legalistic about the evidence of the old title pages and dedicatory epistles. Rights in dramatic authorship were lightly held, and Dekker, who had let Middleton sign the preface to *The Roaring Girl,* would have been the first to encourage Ford to publish the play as he did, and to make what he could from a dedication. In what follows, William Rowley, who may also have been in on the original authorship of *Perkin Warbeck,* must figure as a forgotten man, since his presence or absence does not affect the argument. Our task is to scrutinize the association of Dekker and Ford. That there should ever have been such an association is one of the anomalies of the period, typical of its resistance to our efforts at formulation. We think of Dekker as the robust "Elizabethan" and Ford as the effete "Carolinian," with the difference between them approximating the difference between the lusty springtime of *The Shoemaker's Holiday* and the smoky summer of *The Broken Heart.* Moreover, our impressions are by no means false, any more than our impressions are false that Shakespeare and Fletcher were antithetical, even though for a time they may have been writing associates. It would have been obliging of Dekker and Ford if they had remained aloof in their respective seasons, exchanging wholesome and decadent stares, but actually they disregarded spiritual and social gulfs in the most confusing possible way—by coming together as collaborators. This collaboration was no momentary thing but extended over a considerable period of time and involved a considerable number of plays. Between 1621 and 1624 they collaborated on *The Witch of Edmonton* (with Rowley), *The Sun's Darling, The Fairy Knight, A Late Murther of the Son upon the Mother* (with Webster and Rowley), *The Bristowe Merchant,* and possibly *The Welsh Ambassador.* It would be interesting to review the known facts about all these plays,[5] but limits of space forbid. A few words must be included about the three extant.

The Welsh Ambassador, surviving in manuscript in the Cardiff Public Library, was ascribed to Dekker and Ford on stylistic grounds by Bertram Lloyd in 1945.[6] The ascription is of more than usual interest, since it is confirmed, at least as regards Dekker, by evidence of which Lloyd was unaware. A play called "the Welch Embassador or a Comedy in disguises" is assigned to Dekker in the list of manuscript plays found in the notebook of the collector Abraham Hill (1635–1721).[7] Without recourse to verbal analysis, it is easy to see Dekker in the play but difficult to see Ford. The same thing may be said of *The Sun's Darling,* licensed for the Cockpit on March 3, 1624, as "in the nature of a masque by Deker, and Forde"[8] and published as by them in 1656. It reverts somewhat wearily to devices of moral allegory found in parts of Dekker's *Old Fortunatus.*

The most relevant play of the collaboration is *The Witch of Edmonton,* published in 1658 as "By divers well-esteemed Poets; William Rowley, Thomas Dekker, John Ford, &c." The "&c." suggests that Webster may have been in upon this enterprise as well as upon the *Late Murther.* The title page informs us further that the play was "Acted by the Princes Servants, often at the Cock-Pit in Drury-Lane, once at court, with singular applause." The fact of the court performance is confirmed by a warrant of payment dated December 29,

[5] The facts are expertly presented by Gerald E. Bentley, *Jacobean and Caroline Stage,* vol. III (Oxford, 1956), passim.

[6] "The Authorship of the Welsh Embassador," *Review of English Studies,* 21 (1945), 192–201. The play has been edited by H. Littledale and W. W. Greg, *Malone Society Reprints,* 1920.

[7] J. Q. Adams, "Hill's List of Early Plays in Manuscript," *Library, New Series,* 20 (1939), 86–88.

[8] *Dramatic Records of Sir Henry Herbert,* ed. J. Q. Adams (New Haven, 1917), p. 27.

1621. As previously noted, the play is excellent, homogeneous (by the standards applicable to its type), and different from anything written by its authors singly. However, prodded by the title page, we can most easily detect Dekker, least easily detect Ford.

We know definitely, then, that from at least 1621 until at least 1624 Dekker was collaborating with Ford, sometimes along with others but more frequently with him alone. We know that their plays were usually written for the Cockpit companies. And we know that in the collaboration Dekker's was the informing spirit. Now what is there to suggest that *Perkin Warbeck* may derive from this interlude in the careers of the two men? *The Witch of Edmonton* is based in part upon Henry Goodcole's *The Wonderful Discoverie of Elizabeth Sawyer,* following closely upon the publication of the pamphlet in 1621. *Perkin Warbeck* is based upon Thomas Gainsford's *The True and Wonderfull History of Perkin Warbeck,* 1618, and Francis Bacon's *Historie of the Raigne of King Henry the Seventh,* 1622. It too may have followed closely upon the publication of its sources, since there is no internal evidence in the play dictating a date of composition later than 1622. The character name "Warbeck" appears in *The Witch of Edmonton* but not in its known source, thus suggesting the authors' familiarity with the Gainsford *History.* The Hill list of manuscript plays contains the title *Believe it is so & tis so* by "Th. Decker." This would be an excellent alternate title for *Perkin Warbeck,* which leans heavily upon a suggestion about Warbeck in Bacon: "Nay, himselfe, with long and continuall counterfeiting, and oft telling a Lye, was turned by habite almost into the thing he seemed to bee; and from a Lyer, to a Believer."[9] If there is virtue in Lloyd's proposal that *The*

---

[9] *The Historie of the Raigne of King Henry the Seventh,* p. 120.

Welsh Ambassador (listed by Hill as by Dekker) is actually by Dekker and Ford, there may also be virtue in the proposal, although suggested by its title alone, that *Believe it is so & tis so* (also listed by Hill as by Dekker) may be by Dekker and Ford. At least the title indicates some interest on Dekker's part in the kind of phenomenon that figures so conspicuously in the play we are considering, and it is of the proverbial cast not infrequently found among titles of chronicle plays.

Perkin Warbeck was published in 1634 as "Acted (sometimes) by the Queenes Maiesties Servants at the Phoenix in Drury lane." It is one of seven plays published with dedications by Ford between 1629 and 1639.[10] Five of the seven are, like itself, Cockpit plays, and those that can be dated were written only a year or two before their publication. This would imply that *Perkin Warbeck,* despite the absence of internal evidence, was written about 1631–1633, except for one curious fact: its title page alone among the seven plays employs the word "some-times" in reference to the stage production. The word was used then, as now, in the sense of "occasionally," but if such was the meaning intended, it is difficult to see why it should have been employed at all, since all plays were then acted "occasionally." Certainly one would not advertise the fact that his play was acted *infrequently.* But the word was also used in the sense of "formerly."[11] It seems legitimate to construe the "some-

---

[10] *The Lovers Melancholy,* 1629; *Loves Sacrifice,* 1633; *Tis Pitty Shee's a Whore,* 1633; *The Broken Heart,* 1633; *The Chronicle Historie of Perkin Warbeck,* 1634; *The Fancies Chast and Noble,* 1638; *The Ladies Triall,* 1639. See *John Fordes Dramatische Werke,* ed. W. Bang and H. De Vocht, 2 vols. (Louvaine, 1908, 1927).

[11] O.E.D. gives an illustration from 1627: "There is at this day to be seene a board belonging sometimes to Tullius Cicero (Hakewill Apol. [1630], 374."

times" of the title page as meaning that *Perkin Warbeck,* unlike the other six plays, was not new at the time of publication. This title page permits us to place the date of its performance as early as 1625 since Queen Henrietta's Men had occupied the Phoenix (i.e., Cockpit) since that date; hence it might have followed closely upon the known series of Cockpit plays written by Dekker and Ford between 1621 and 1624.

Of course nothing that has been said above provides evidence that *Perkin Warbeck* was written in collaboration by Dekker and Ford. The facts are merely permissive, or at best merely suggestive. Let us turn now to the play itself. I should like to invite the reader to reexamine, with the possibility of a Dekker-Ford collaboration in mind, the second scene of the play. The humorous old Earl of Huntley is warning the daughter, whom he dearly loves, and the young lord, whom he truly likes, that reasons of state virtually forbid their marriage. There is nothing in the style to rule out Ford; in fact, when Huntley speaks merely as a sarcastic and peremptory father, his lines resemble those of some other fathers in Ford. For instance:

> ... well young Lord
> This will not doe yet, if the girle be headstrong
> And will not harken to good Counsaile, steale her
> And runne away with her, daunce galliards, doe,
> And friske about the world to learn the languages:
> T'will be a thriving trade; you may set vp by't.

This is not unlike the scolding of Croton in the first scene of *The Broken Heart:*

> Athens? pray why to Athens? you intend not
> To kicke against the world, turne Cynicke, Stoicke,
> Or read the Logicke Lecture, or become
> An Areopagite; and Iudge in causes

> Touching the Common-wealth? for as I take it
> The budding of your chin cannot prognosticate
> So grave an honour.

But what of a speech such as the following?

> I scorne not thy affection to my Daughter,
> Not I by good St. Andrew; but this bugg-beare,
> This whoresome tale of honor, (*honor* Daliell)
> So hourely chatts and tattles in mine eare,
> The piece of royaltie that is stich'd vp
> In my Kates bloud, that 'tis as dangerous
> For thee young Lord, to perch so neere an Eaglet,
> As foolish for my gravitie to admit it.
> I have spoake all at once.

If we came upon this speech in isolation, would we not guess that it was written by Dekker rather than by Ford?

And yet the speeches in isolation provide the weakest support for my argument. It is rather the whole conception of the scene, and the nature of the author's participation in it, that spell Dekker to me rather than Ford. Old Huntley, tough without and tender within, making humorous asides (both natural and genuinely funny), jostled between love and admiration, between generous impulse and shrewd caution, is unlike anything elsewhere in Ford but like many things elsewhere in Dekker. The best that Ford could do with the love-relationship of father and daughter is represented in the Meleander-Eroclea scenes in *The Lovers Melancholy*, with their reminiscences of Shakespeare. What Dekker could do with it is represented by the Friscobaldo-Bellafront scenes in 2 *Honest Whore*, while humorous old men were his specialty. In consequence, he is taken by common consent to be the creator of old Carter in *The Witch of Edmonton*. When the latter comes upon the murdered body of his beloved daughter, he dazedly berates it:

> When I speak I look to be spoken to:
> Forgetful slut!

Here we get one of those startling flashes of insight found only in the old drama at its best. When Huntley learns that his daughter will meet the obligations imposed by her birth, his words ring with a like authenticity:

> Kate, Kate, thou grow'st vpon my heart, like peace,
> Creating every other houre a Iubile.

I doubt if Ford could have imagined this scene, and I do not believe that he did.

Dekker, yes—but Dekker under restraints. It would have been characteristic of him to let Lady Katherine Gordon be accompanied on her pilgrimage, not by Lord Daliell but by an incongruous comic groom, such as Shadow in *Old Fortunatus* or Babulo in *Patient Grissel,* dubious about the alleged royalty of her husband but doggedly faithful to her. This clown would have engaged in a running campaign of persiflage with Warbeck's lowborn "councilors," one of whom unquestionably would have baffled us with Dekker's version of Irish or Welsh dialect. But I have already pointed out that *Perkin Warbeck* was a tour de force, consciously based upon the best models of a dramatic genre that had passed from fashion. It most nearly resembles *Richard II,* which illustrated that even Shakespeare could forego clowning, and let even gardeners speak with an unwonted decorum. Let us say that Dekker was placed on his best behavior. Why, then, should not this line of reasoning apply equally to Ford, producing a tour de force alone? Again the answer must take the form of a question: What would Ford defer to as invoking his "best behavior"? I can only say that the departures of the play from Dekker's norm are superficial, while its departures from Ford's are fundamental. I shall return to the point in conclusion.

My belief that Dekker wrote part of *Perkin Warbeck* and shaped the play as a whole is, of course, impressionistic. But in view of the variety of collaborative methods that there must have been, resulting at least sometimes in the conceptions of one author underlying the words of another, we dare not restrict ourselves to the application of verbal tests, useful though those often are. In certain instances impressions may be more reliable than an analysis of the incidence of "d'ee" and "d'ye." Some years ago I argued that Ford was the original author of *The Duke of Lerma,* prepared by Robert Howard for the Restoration stage. Only one of the critics of Ford has dismissed my case out of hand, while another has proposed that the play be incorporated in future editions. This, although gratifying, is in excess of my expectations when I discussed the play; and I have but fluttering hopes indeed that Fredson Bowers will include *Perkin Warbeck* in his current edition of Dekker. I am not really trying to establish property rights in these plays. But neither am I playing a game of give-and-take simply to create a disturbance. It strikes me that the only value that discussions of authorship can have resides in their clarification of critical issues, and in their encouraging us to come to decisions about what individual authors were like.

T. S. Eliot has written no essay on Dekker, but he has praised several of his conceptions almost by inadvertence— Moll Frith in his discussion of the merits of Middleton, and Cuddie Banks in his discussion of the defects of Heywood.[12] His high estimate of *Perkin Warbeck* may be another instance. There is something about Dekker that Eliot likes, and he would not be dismayed by the charge. However, the critics

---

[12] *Selected Essays,* pp. 167, 177–78. Eliot supposed Moll to be the creation of Middleton, which seems unlikely, and Cuddie to be the creation of Dekker, which seems less unlikely, although most scholars have credited the character to William Rowley.

who feel less secure might find it convenient if we were able to settle certain problems of authorship so that they might rest assured that they were praising and damning the right people. The whirligig of critical fashion has thrust Dekker down as it has thrust Ford up. L. C. Knights has said, "with a few exceptions Dekker's plays are uniformly dull, and the effort of attention they require—the sheer effort to keep one's eyes on the page—is out of all proportion to the reward."[13] To me this is one of the most incomprehensible literary judgments of our time, but I am sure that many approve it. These are invited to blame the defects of *Perkin Warbeck* upon Dekker. It lacks, we repeatedly hear, Ford's typical intensity. Well, Dekker was notoriously lacking in intensity.

Dekker was lacking in other gifts possessed by Ford. Although declared by the most generous of all good critics to have "poetry enough for anything," he had not poetry enough to write like Ford, nor did he have Ford's power to produce an almost hypnotic dramatic effect. But Dekker possessed certain gifts that Ford had been denied. He was, for one thing, a better playwright. To watch Dekker getting a play under way is a lesson in craftsmanship. In the first two hundred lines of *The Shoemaker's Holiday* he establishes immediate interest, sets a situation, provides for future developments, creates and qualifies our sense of social antagonisms, writes language of great vitality (at times interspersed with sallets to keep the matter savory), and rounds the action off with a parade of Londoners to the French wars in a way that is at once stirring, comical, and touching—and all with such an appearance of ease as to make the unwary reader say, "Why, this is nothing at all." Meanwhile he has introduced and differentiated ten major and minor characters. It is not only that we come to know what Simon Eyre is like—shrewd

---

[13] *Drama and Society in the Age of Jonson* (London, 1951), p. 228.

exploiter of his own eccentricities—but that we know just as well what his three journeymen, Firk, Hodge, and Ralph, are like; indeed, so well that our texts might just as well omit their speech prefixes thereafter. It is not an easy thing to do. Marlowe was a great writer, but we are unable to distinguish among Tamburlaine's three journeymen, Techelles, Theridamus, and Usamcasane, after ten full acts.

All will concede, I believe, the awkwardness of Ford's structural devices, and the colorlessness of his minor characters. His inferiority to Dekker in another department will be granted with no such unanimity. Indeed, even to mention it as an inferiority lays one open to grave charges of moralism, even of Americanism. M. Joan Sargeaunt has said, "To turn from the sincere artistic appreciation of Taine and Havelock Ellis or the open attacks of Hazlitt to the puritanical upbraidings of the American critics of the first decade of the present century is to take a backward plunge,"[14] whereupon she quotes Schelling as a scold and cites Thorndike as a prude. This is what we have come to recognize as "loaded" language. After carefully rereading the criticism mentioned, I fail to detect where the comment of Schelling and Thorndike is less "sincere" than that of Taine and Ellis, or their expressed disapproval less "open" than that of Hazlitt. I should not classify Hazlitt's comment as an "attack," or agreement with it as a "backward plunge." I find less scolding in Schelling than in Miss Sargeaunt, and less naïveté in Thorndike than in her assumption that certain criteria are applicable only to works found "in the nursery." However, all this is beside the point. What is really important is the veiled implication that disapproval of Ford must have its origin in the limitations of those who disapprove. Eliot has shaken off the curse of his national origins so that his response is merely strange: "Mr.

---

[14] *John Ford*, p. 184.

Eliot seems strangely to have missed the significance of Ford's plays."

What Miss Sargeaunt fails to point out is that the disapproval of certain aspects of Ford's work expressed by Schelling was expressed in almost identical terms by A. W. Ward[15] in the standard work on the drama current in England in the period mentioned. The nature of the summing up in the comment upon Ford by such writers as Ward and Schelling is not owing to their nationality, creed, or period, but to their efforts as historians to portray English Renaissance drama as a whole, and each part of it in perspective. They assumed that if Shakespeare's works were the finest product of this dramatic era, as all agree that they were, then the qualities found in his works might be used as a measure of the value of the qualities found in the works of others. A playwright achieved stature to the extent that he resembled Shakespeare. We need not accept this assumption, and indeed much may be said against it, but we should recognize that Ford has benefited from it in some respects—no one's language has more often been praised as "Shakespearean." In other respects he has failed to benefit.

This ground has been gone over so often that I shall not linger upon it. In Shakespeare there is an overall consistency in the selection and emphasis of material that validates, in the only acceptable way in which it can be validated, the principle of the *dulce et utile* as applied to art. Evidently Shakespeare deemed it useless to dwell on certain things. The spectacle of Juliet sadly accepting Paris while letting Romeo go might be more sweet than useful: Patience upon a monument smiling at grief might be worth a metaphor but not a tragedy. And the unattainability or the evanescence of ideal love

[15] *A History of English Dramatic Literature*, 3 vols. (London, 1899), III, 88–89.

Swift as a shadow, short as any dream,
Brief as the lightning in the collied night

stood as an "edict in destiny." To the inventory of its hazards, long and formidable enough, consanguinity need not be added, since the limited applicability of this hazard as compared with the others might somewhat obscure the issue. All dreams and all shapes of dreams were known to Shakespeare, but not all seemed of equal value, and we are the beneficiaries of his principle of selection: it belittles his work to call it bracing, but it is never marred by an enervating sentimentalism.

With Ford the case is different. One may properly argue that the difference is of small aesthetic consequence, and one grows irritated with critics only when they maintain in the same breath that the difference is of small consequence and that it does not exist. Ford, they insist, is himself an idealist. He is indeed, but he does not discriminate between invigorating and enervating dreams. He more nearly resembles Tennessee Williams than William Shakespeare.

Dekker more nearly resembles Shakespeare. He was simpler than Shakespeare (although not simple), and his objectives may be stated in simpler terms. He wanted to make a living by entertaining and to do some incidental good. L. C. Knights charged that his morality was a mechanical reflex, representing little more than a line of least resistance. I think he might decide otherwise if he would read all of Dekker and succeed in what he has called the "sheer effort" of keeping his eyes on the page. *Northward Hoe* and *Westward Hoe* come closest to deviation, but the wonder is that in everything else, and in a measure even in these, Dekker clung to certain principles no matter with whom or for whom he wrote. He could impose them upon Middleton and he could impose them upon Ford. He was, said Jonson, a rogue, and in the Jonsonian sense of taking a rather cavalier view of his responsibilities as an artist, he really was so. Yet in spite of his carelessness, his bumptiousness, his repetitiousness, his too ready vein of ribaldry, he kept the faith in something essential. Like Shakespeare he never appealed to moral weakness.

The treatment of the career of Lady Katherine Gordon, which appears on first glance to be the most Fordian element in the play before us, proves actually to be the least. Both Dekker and Ford have portrayed independently a number of wives victimized by their marriages, but here the similarity ends. In no play of Dekker is the suffering of such a woman, or indeed of anyone, invested with appeal per se. In the case of Lady Katherine the stress is not upon gentle resignation to misfortune, but upon the assertion of a principle—that of marital fidelity. Thus she is nearer kin to Dekker's Bellafront than to Ford's Calantha. Dekker wrote some bad plays—he was a rogue—but he also wrote some remarkably good ones, and as long as he continued to fill up sheets and to parcel out jobs to younger collaborators, he preserved at least one Shakespearean ingredient in the drama. I believe that his parting gift to it may be the mysteriously firm moral texture of *The Chronicle Historie of Perkin Warbeck. A Strange Truth.*

$\mathcal{M}$Y HYPOTHESIS may be briefly stated: Certain playwrights after 1660 secured, in manuscript, unprinted plays written before 1642, modernized them, and had them produced and published as their own; hence a number of Restoration plays which pass with us as original are actually adaptations of "lost" Elizabethan and Stuart plays. If my argument holds, some of the pilferers as well as the pilfered prove notable figures in literary history, and to the shades of the former I offer a word of propitiation. Although my terms and methods suggest police investigation, I am bringing no criminal charges, or at least no charges of felony. To appropriate silently the work of earlier playwrights was in former times an accepted practice. Theatrical companies rather than playwrights held title to plays, and recognized no impediment, legal or moral, to letting new writers refurbish old writing and thus preserve it for the repertories. How many of the plays we assign, let us say, to Jacobean playwrights are reworkings of plays by Elizabethans we do not know, but it is certain that there are some.

MOTIVE

Known practices of the Restoration supply us with a kind of a priori case. Restoration drama is extremely derivative. Between 1660 and 1700 somewhat fewer than five hundred and fifty "new" plays were produced or written with pro-

This article, developed from a suggestion I made in a paper read at a Modern Language Association meeting in December 1936, was originally printed in the *Modern Language Review,* vol. 35 (1940).

duction in mind. Of these, over forty were translations or adaptations of foreign plays and over sixty were adaptations of older English plays.[1] Among the adapters were Davenant, Dryden, Sedley, Tuke, Digby, Villiers, Rochester, Shadwell, Betterton, Behn, Settle, Otway, Ravenscroft, D'Urfey, Crown, Tate, and Vanbrugh. Those adapted were chiefly Corneille and Molière among the foreign playwrights, Shakespeare and Fletcher among the native, but the list of the latter includes also Webster, Massinger, Hemming, Brome, Middleton, Brewer, Marston, Marmion, William Rowley, Chapman, Shirley, and even Marlowe and Jonson. Over a hundred plays, nearly a fifth of the total, are demonstrably unoriginal. Excluded from the count are the "drolls" derived from pre-Commonwealth drama, and scholarly translations from classical drama such as those by Echard, Sherburne, and others. The word "adaptation" has been loosely used in histories of the drama, and in the case of a few plays which I have not read my authorities may have deceived me, but I have tried to exclude from the count plays which merely lean upon precursors for characters, plots, and occasional details. The one hundred and six are sufficiently close to their originals to have made, even according to the easygoing standards of the day, some kind of acknowledgment appropriate—or so we should suppose.

By no means, however, was the acknowledgment generally forthcoming. In some cases the conscience of adapter or printer, or both, proved robust beyond belief. Titles were altered and readers were supplied no hint of the existence of original versions. In 1661 James Shirley's *Constant Maid,*

---

[1] The count is based upon my analytical play-list, *Annals of English Drama, 975-1700,* which was going through the press at the time this article was written. This book has been thoroughly revised by Samuel Schoenbaum (London, Methuen, 1964), but I do not believe the statistics are materially affected.

first issued in 1640, was reissued as *Love will find out the Way* by "T. B."—this while the original author was still alive. An adaptation of Shirley's *The Traitor* was printed in 1692. The original title was retained, but the dedicatee, the Earl of Clancarty, Baron Blarney, was informed that for this play, "one of the best Tragedies that this Age hath Produced . . . it is Commendation enough to say the Author was Mr Rivers." Even such close translations as William Lower's *Amorous Fantasm*,[2] 1660, and Davenant's *The Man's the Master*,[3] 1669, were published without hint of their true nature. There was point to John Caryl's Epilogue to *Sir Salomon, or The Cautious Coxcomb*,[4] 1671:

> What we have brought before you, was not meant
> For a new Play, but a new President;
> For we with Modesty our Theft avow,
> (There is some Conscience shewn in stealing too)
> And openly declare, that if our Cheer
> Does hit your Pallats, you must thank Molliere:

An examination of the title pages, prefatory material, prologues, and epilogues of most of the translations and adaptations of the period enables me to make certain generalizations. We must notice, first of all, that the publishers were quite ruthless: rare, indeed, was the title page that signaled to the purchaser that the play was secondhand. The playwrights were also ruthless, but somewhat more careful. Renderings from Pierre Corneille (though not from Thomas) were usually admitted, and also, as his reputation grew, were those from Molière. Adaptations of Shakespeare and Fletcher usu-

---

[2] Quinault's *Le Fantôme amoureux.*

[3] Scarron's *Jodelet, ou le maître valet.* Both *The Man's the Master* and *The Rivals* (unacknowledged adaptation of *Two Noble Kinsmen*) were published after Davenant's death, so that his responsibility is limited.

[4] Adaptation of *L'École des femmes*, etc., acted 1669–1670.

ally confess themselves to be such, sometimes naming the original author, sometimes assuming him to be known. Frequently, however, the admission is quite inconspicuous, and the debt is minimized. For his *Fool's Preferment*,[5] 1688, D'Urfey confesses only to a "hint" from Fletcher; and for *The Unhappy Kindness*,[6] 1697, Scott to "little . . . but the Design." Never is the original play a subject to be dwelt upon.

Corneille, Molière, Shakespeare, and Fletcher were so well known that wholesale appropriation was simply impracticable. With the lesser-known writers the case was otherwise. We have already noticed that James Shirley's plays seemed "safe." Other instances are provided by Davenant's *The Rivals*, 1668 (Two Noble Kinsmen); Behn's (?) *The Debauchee*, 1677 (Brome's *Mad Couple Well Matched*); Behn's (?) *The Counterfeit Bridegroom*, 1677 (Middleton's *No Wit No Help like a Woman's*); Leanerd's *The Country Innocence*, 1677 (Brewer's *Country Girl*); Leanerd's *Rambling Justice*, 1678 (Middleton's *More Dissemblers besides Women*); Tate's *A Duke and No Duke*, 1685 (Cokain's *Trappolin Supposed a Prince*); Anonymous, *The Rampant Alderman*, 1685 (Marmion's *Fine Companion*); Harris's *The City Bride*, 1696 (Webster's *Cure for a Cuckold*). These are all adaptations parading as original plays. The list is merely illustrative, and is limited to plays with English originals in print.

Unless the older play is famous, mention of indebtedness is so rare as to seem gratuitous. D'Urfey's dedication of his version of *Bussy D'Ambois*, 1691, contains a patronizing allusion to Chapman; and Settle's *Love and Revenge*,[7] 1675, curi-

---

[5] Adapted from *The Noble Gentleman*.

[6] Adapted from Fletcher's *Wife for a Month*.

[7] Acted 1674. Settle takes for granted that Guarini will be known as original author of *Pastor Fido*, adapted by him in 1677, but he is misleading on the subject of *Herod and Mariamne*, which he published in 1674 with the comment that the play (Corneille's) "was given him by a

ously indeed, pays proper tribute to Hemming's *Fatal Contract*. Shadwell is one of the more frank adapters of the period, but whether he deserves credit for describing *The Royal Shepherdess*, 1669, as an adaptation of Fountain's *Rewards of Virtue* depends somewhat upon whether Fountain was still alive. An amusing instance of enforced candor is provided by Aphra Behn's *The Rover*, Part I, 1677: the "Postscript" reads in part: "This play had been sooner in Print, but for a Report about the Town (made by some either very Malitious or very Ignorant) that 'twas *Thomaso* alter'd; which made the Book-sellers fear some trouble from the Proprietor of that Admirable Play, which indeed has Wit enough to stock a Poet. . . ." Amidst additional sweet words for Killigrew, author of *Thomaso*, Mrs. Behn remarks that she has "stol'n some hints." And indeed she has! The playwrights sometimes resort to simple ambiguity: Tate's Epilogue to *Injured Love*, 1707, reads in part:

> One could with less Expence i'th' Modern Way,
> Have fitted out a slight New-fashioned Play
> To Leak, and Bulge, and Founder in the Bay;
> But chose a Vessel that would bear the shock
> Of censure; yes, old Built, but Heart of Oak.

These lines would pacify the knowledgeable, given to browsing in old quartos, but would scarcely inform the average citizen that *Injured Love* is an adaptation of Webster's *The White Devil*.

At the moment my case stands as follows: Restoration playwrights frequently *did* adapt pre-Restoration plays, and, when it seemed safe to do so, adapted them surreptitiously. Existence of the parent play was mentioned reluctantly or not at

---

gentleman." The mysterious "gentleman" who gives away plays will be encountered again.

all. Yet the parent plays thus far mentioned were all in print. Had they come to the adapters in manuscript, we might predicate a uniform and penetrating silence. And what about plays in manuscript? The adapters would not have confined themselves to printed plays were others available. Unprinted plays would have served just as well those who were writing for money, and would have served much better those who were writing for fame.

OPPORTUNITY

I have been discussing Motive: what follows is *de rigueur*. Granted that Restoration writers were willing to utilize plays in manuscript, would they have been able to do so? The answer is unequivocal. Scores of manuscripts were available. Between 1558 and 1642, so many plays were left unprinted that our lists, even though incomplete, record the titles of hundreds. That the manuscripts of many of the unprinted plays survived to the Restoration is indicated by the number that have survived to the present day.[8] But concern with these would be self-defeating: our immediate problem is a practical one. The present phase of my discussion I shall limit to known manuscripts—*now lost but not lost in 1660,* and distinguished then by their concentration in collections of noticeable size and by their probable accessibility to the new playwrights.

On 29 December 1653, the bookseller Richard Marriott entered in the Stationers' Register the titles of twenty-one plays. The names of the authors were not given, but, judging by the modish titles, most of the plays belonged to the decade before 1642. Only two of Marriott's plays were published, the manuscripts of the rest presumably remaining in the shop

[8] I have attempted to catalogue these in *PMLA,* 50 (1935), 687–699; 52 (1937), 905–907; 53 (1938), 624–629. (The list has been amplified in *Annals of English Drama* [1964], 307–322.)

where he conducted his business well into the Restoration period. That booksellers kept play manuscripts in stock is proved by Francis Kirkman's note to his catalogue of plays appended to *All Mistaken, or The Mad Couple,* 1672: "Although there are but 806 Playes in all Printed, yet I know that many more have been Written and Acted, I myself have some quantity in Manuscript." At some time between 1677 and 1703 Abraham Hill, antiquarian and bibliophile, took down the titles of a collection of manuscript plays—quite possibly Kirkman's. Hill's list contains over fifty titles, most of them belonging to the early part of the century and otherwise unknown.[9]

For our purpose, the most significant collection of manuscripts was that made by the enterprising publisher Humphrey Moseley late in the Interregnum. On 9 September 1653, and 29 June 1660, Moseley entered in the Stationers' Register the titles of from eighty to ninety plays.[10] Had Moseley lived, he might have issued many of these plays, possibly even a Massinger folio, but death intervened and only eighteen of the plays ever found their way into print. What happened to the rest is suggested by the following sequence of events.

In the early spring of 1660 it had become apparent that the theatres were to become legitimate once more. On 29 June, Moseley effected the second, precautionary, registration of his collection, rectifying most of the many double entries for single fees made in 1653. On 30 August he wrote to Sir Henry Herbert, Master of the Revels, as follows:

[9] J. Q. Adams, "Hill's List of Early Plays in Manuscript," *Library,* New Series, 20 (1939), 71–99. Dr. Adams kindly sent me his article before publication.

[10] An accurate count is impossible because of the difficulty in distinguishing between two plays entered for a single fee and single plays with double titles. For an analysis of the list, see W. W. Greg, "The Bakings of Betsy," *Library,* Third Series, 2 (1911), 225–259.

Sir,

I have beene very much solicited by the gentlemen actors of the Red Bull for a note under my hand to certifie unto your worship what agreement I had made with Mr Rhodes of the Cockpitt playhouse. Truly, Sir, I am so farr from any agreement with him, that I never so much as treated with him nor with any from him, neither did I ever consent directly or indirectly, that hee or any others should act any playes that doe belong to mee, without my knowledge and consent had and procured. And the same also I doe certify concerning the Whitefryers playhouse and players.

Sir, this is all I have to trouble you withall att present, and therefore I shall take the boldnesse to remaine,

Your Worsh. most humble Servant
Humphrey Mosely[11]

It is evident that Moseley's collection was known and that the newly forming theatrical companies were interested in his plays as a possible part of their repertories. Moseley was on guard, but his health was failing. Elected one of the wardens of the Stationers' Company, 7 July 1659, he never attended a meeting of the Court,[12] and on 31 January 1661 he died.

Moseley's will appoints his "deare and loveing wife Anne Moseley . . . and dutiful Child and onely daughter Anne Mosley" joint executrices, and legatees of "bookes Coppies or Coppies of bookes whatsoever." His servant John Langford was willed £5 provided "hee abideth with my wife dureinge her shopkeepinge . . . to assist her in her great busines"; and his servant Henry Penton the same sum under the same conditions.[13] Anne Moseley did no publishing after

[11] Edmond Malone, *Historical Account of the Rise and Progress of the English Stage,* (London, 1800), p. 311.

[12] Stationers' Company, Records of the Court of Assistants, Liber D, 1654/5-1679, passim.

[13] P.C.C. May 46. Moseley's estate was not great. His brother Thomas Moseley, apothecary of Christchurch, London, states in his will that Hum-

her husband's death, but she conducted the shop at least until 1672, appealing for protection several times to the Court of the Stationers' Company,[14] and at intervals transferring to others, usually Henry Herringman, her rights to printed plays. The present officials of the Honorable Company have permitted me to have the Records of the Court of Assistants searched, but neither there nor elsewhere is there mention of the collection of manuscript plays.

One of two things probably occurred. Either the theatrical groups, those negotiating with Moseley in August 1660, or their successors, secured the manuscripts and failed to use them (the great majority proving unsuitable in unadapted form for stage production after 1660), or else the plays simply remained in Anne Moseley's shop. In either case the probability is great that individual plays would find their way into the hands of Restoration writers. Years later, John Warburton, Somerset Herald, listed thirty-one of the Moseley plays among the manuscripts burnt by his cook. Whether Warburton ever actually possessed all the manuscripts he listed has been questioned,[15] but it seems probable that a residuum of Anne Moseley's stock survived until the eighteenth century and passed into Warburton's hands *en bloc*. Below I list

phrey owes him £225. (Will made 1 Dec. 1660, P.C.C. May 49.) Anne, lacking capital to publish plays, would have been the more ready to realize on manuscripts.

[14] Liber D, 1654/5–1679, ff. 72, 138, 139. Her last transaction with Herringman, so far as I have discovered, is recorded in the Stationers' Register, 14 Oct. 1672.

[15] W. W. Greg, "The Bakings of Betsy," 258–259. I have noted an additional reason to doubt Warburton's claim ("Notes on Manuscript Plays," *TLS*, 20 June 1936, p. 523), but I am inclined to believe now that he did possess all the plays he listed: my findings in the present investigation tend to bear out that supposition. (A recent article by John Freehafer, "John Warburton's Lost Plays," *Studies in Bibliography*, 23 [1970], argues Warburton's veracity.)

the Moseley, Marriott, Hill (Kirkman ?) lost manuscripts, indicating by a (W) those claimed by Warburton for his collection. The list is somewhat long simply to be placed in evidence; I include it for its bearing upon the discussion of individual playwrights to follow, and as a convenience to those who may wish to carry on investigations of their own.

Beaumont	History of Madon, King of Britain	Moseley
Beaumont and Fletcher	A Right Woman	Moseley
Brome	The Lovesick Maid, or The Honor of Young Ladies (Two plays?)	Moseley
Brome	Wit in Madness	Moseley
Brome and Chapman	Christianetta, or Marriage and Hanging go by Destiny	Hill
Brome and Heywood[16]	The Apprentice's Prize	Moseley
	Life and Death of Sir Martin Skink, with the Wars of the Low Countries	Moseley
"Buc, G."	The Ambitious Brother	Hill
Chapman	The Fatal Love (T.)	Moseley (W)
Chapman	A Yorkshire Gentlewoman and her Son (T.)	Moseley (W)
Chettle	All is not Gold that Glisters	Hill
Davenport	The Fatal Brothers (T.)	Moseley
Davenport	The Politic Queen, or Murder will Out (Two plays?)	Moseley
Davenport and Shakespeare	Henry I	Moseley (W)
Davenport and Shakespeare	Henry II	Moseley
Dekker	Gustavus King of Swethland	Moseley (W)
Dekker	Joconda and Astolso (C.)	Moseley (W)
Dekker	The Jew of Venice	Moseley
Dekker	Believe it is so and 'tis so	Hill
Dekker	Disguises, or Love in Disguise, a Petticoat Voyage	Hill
Dekker	The White Moor	Hill
Ford	Beauty in a Trance (C.)	Moseley (W)
Ford	The London Merchant (C.)	Moseley (W)
Ford	A Bad (or Good) Beginning may have a Good Ending (C.)	Moseley (W)
Glapthorne	The Noble Husbands ("Actors Cataloche, le Dirard etc.")	Hill
Glapthorne	The Vestal (T.)	Moseley (W)
Glapthorne	The Noble Trial (T. or T.C.)	Moseley (W)
Glapthorne	The Duchess of Fernandina (T.)	Moseley (W)
Lane, Philip	A Christmas Tale, or The Knight and the Cobbler	Hill
Le Grys	Nothing Impossible to Love (T.C.)	Moseley (W)
Jordan	Love hath found his Eyes	Moseley (W)

Marmion (or Bonen)	The Crafty Merchant	Moseley (W)
Massinger	The Painter	Moseley
Massinger	The Italian Nightpiece	Moseley
Massinger	The Unfortunate Piety	Moseley
Massinger	The Tyrant (T.)	Moseley (W)
Massinger	Philenzo and Hypollita (T.C.)	Moseley (W)
Massinger	Antonio and Vallia (C.)	Moseley (W)
Massinger	Fast and Welcome (C.)	Moseley (W)
Massinger	Alexis the Chaste Gallant	Moseley (W)
Massinger	The Woman's Plot	Moseley (W)
Massinger	The Judge	Moseley (W)
Massinger	The Spanish Viceroy	Moseley
Massinger	The Honor of Women (C.)	Moseley (W)
Massinger	Minerva's Sacrifice	Moseley (W)
Massinger (?)	The Forced Lady (T.)	Moseley (W)
Massinger	The Fair Anchoress [of Pausilippo]	Moseley
Massinger	The City Honest Man	Moseley
Massinger (?)	The Orator	Moseley
Massinger (?)	The Noble Choice (T.C.)	Moseley
Middleton	The Conqueror's Custom, or The Fair Prisoner	Hill
Middleton	The Puritan Maid, Modest Wife, and Wanton Widow	Moseley (W)
Rowley, W.	The Nonesuch (C.)	Moseley (W)
Rowley, W.	The Four Honorable Lovers (C.)	Moseley (W)
Rowley, W.	The Fool without Book	Moseley
Rowley, W.	A Knave in Print, or One for Another (Two plays?)	Moseley
Sampson, W.	The Widow's Prize[17]	Moseley (W)
Shakespeare[18]	Duke Humphrey (T.)	Moseley (W)
Shakespeare	The History of King Stephen	Moseley
Shakespeare	Iphis and Ianthe, or Marriage without a Man (Two plays?)	Moseley
Shakespeare and Fletcher	The History of Cardenio	Moseley
Shirley, H.	The Dumb Bawd	Moseley
Shirley, H.	The Duke of Guise	Moseley
Shirley, H.	Giraldo, the Constant Lover	Moseley
Shirley, H.	The Spanish Duke of Lerma	Moseley
Tourneur	The Nobleman (T.C.)	Moseley (W)
Tourneur	The Great Man (T.)	Moseley (W)

(In the remaining plays the author is not listed.)

The Black Wedding	Marriott
The Bond Woman	Marriott
Castara, or Cruelty without Hate	Marriott
The Cloudy Queen and Singing Moor	Hill
The Conceits	Marriott
The Country Man	Moseley

A Court Purge	Hill
The Divorce	Marriott
The Dutch Painter and the French Brawl	Hill
The Eunuch (T.)	Marriott
The False Friend	Hill
The Fatal Banquet	Hill
The Florentine Friend	Marriott
A Fool and her Maidenhead soon Parted	Marriott
A Gentleman no Gentleman, a Metamorphosed Courtier ("Actors Eustace, Frampole, Friswood, etc.")	Hill
The King's Mistress	Moseley
Look on me and Love me, or Marriage in the Dark	Hill
Love's Infancy	Hill
The Lover's Holiday, or The Bear	Hill
The Marriage Night	Hill
A Match without Money, or The Wife's Prize	Hill
More than Nine Days Wonder: Two Constant Women	Hill
Mull Sack, or The Looking Glass, the Bachelor, or the Hawk	Hill
The Noble Ravishers	Marriott
The Painted Lady	Hill
Philip of Macedon	Hill
Pity the Maid	Marriott
The Politic Bankrupt, or Which is the Best Girl (Two plays?)	Moseley
The Proxy, or Love's Aftergame	Marriott
Salisbury Plain (C.)	Marriott
Spanish Preferment	Hill
The Supposed Inconstancy	Marriott
Tereus with a Pastoral ("Actors Agnostus, Eupathus, etc. Actors Mufti, Nassuf, etc.")	Hill
Tradeways's Tragedy	Hill
The Tragedy of Tomerania	Hill
The Triumph of Innocence	Hill
The Two Spanish Gentlemen	Hill
The Unfaithful Wife	Hill
The Wandering Jew	Hill
A Way to make a Knave Honest	Hill
The White Witch of Westminster, or Love in a Lunacy	Hill
The Widow Captain	Hill
The Woman's Law	Marriott

The Woman's Masterpiece	Marriott
The Wronged Widow's Tragedy	Hill
The Younger Brother	Marriott
The Younger Brother, or Male Courtesan	Hill

Since Hill's list was made after 1677, the titles indicated as his are significant for our purpose only in relation to late Restoration drama. In the case of the Moseley plays, the greater interest attaches to the titles *not* listed by Warburton, since Warburton must have acquired a group of plays that had survived the process of attrition. Of course, any of the plays listed above may have existed in additional copies.

For the moment I shall beg the question. Is it likely that Marriott, Kirkman, or Anne Moseley would have possessed such stores of manuscript plays without either publishing them or calling the attention of producers and playwrights to them—in a theatrical era much given to reviving or adapting plays coeval in origin with those in manuscript? Or is it likely in an age when the reopening of the theatres forced playwrights to learn their craft rapidly, when gentle but unqualified amateurs aspired to be sealed of the tribe of playhouse wits, and when professional writers were both predatory and furtive, that no use would be made of the opportunity offered? Let us believe the lesser wonder.

That the hypothesis offered here has come tardily forth is no argument against it. The very process of adapting manuscripts would have removed them from circulation and thus concealed traces. The nature of the unacknowledged adaptations previously discussed is known only as a result of literary

[16] The two Brome and Heywood titles were entered in the Register by Moseley, 8 April 1654; and another play by Brome, *The Jewish Gentleman,* was entered 4 Aug. 1640.

[17] In the Hill list occurs *The Widow's Prize, or The Woman Captain.*

[18] See also under Davenport. Warburton listed, in addition to *Henry I* and *Duke Humphrey,* "A Play by Will Shakespear."

discovery, extending over many years and dependent upon the separate existence of printed parent plays. Had there been no prints there would have been no discoveries, and the adaptations would remain unsuspected. The pioneer in such discoveries wrote that he would expose "our Modern Plagiaries by detecting *Part* of their Thefts. I say *Part* because I cannot be suppos'd to have trac'd them in All."[19] Perhaps he spoke more truly than he knew. It is amusing to think of playwrights, secure in their use of manuscript sources, laughing up their sleeves at Langbaine. It is even more amusing to imagine Langbaine's listing, as the sources of an adapted play, the sources of the parent play—in works which the adapter had never heard of. How humiliating to find oneself diminished from thief to receiver! Something of the sort may sometimes have occurred. At any rate, I am sure that some Restoration plays are unrecognized adaptations of "lost" Elizabethan plays, simply on the basis of antecedent probabilities, without reference to particular instances. However, I shall try to indicate possible instances.

CLUE

One of the Moseley manuscripts has furnished the substance for a cause célèbre. The case is so nearly parallel to those I shall argue that a brief review of it will make my claims seem less abrupt.

In the Christmas season of 1612-13 the King's Men presented at Court "Cardenno," and on 8 June 1613 "Cardenna" for the entertainment of the Savoyard ambassador. Entered by Humphrey Moseley in the Stationers' Register, 9 September 1653, was "The History of Cardennio by Mr Fletcher & Shakespeare." The ascription of authorship is fairly credible

[19] G. Langbaine, "The Preface," *An Account of the English Dramatick Poets* (1691).

in view of the collaboration of Fletcher and Shakespeare in 1613. *Cardennio* may have been excluded from the 1623 folio (like *The Two Noble Kinsmen,* published as by Shakespeare and Fletcher in 1634) because mainly the work of the lesser collaborator. No more is heard of the play until there appeared *Double Falsehood, or The Distrest Lover Written Originally by W. Shakespeare, And now Revised and Adapted to the Stage By Mr. Theobald,* acted at Drury Lane in 1727, published the following year. It is the Cardennio story, based, according to the author, upon a Shakespearean manuscript in his possession.

Theobald's claim has been often discussed, in varying tones of belief and disbelief; there is no need to review the controversy. Although *Double Falsehood* itself is not very interesting, it is, in a wide application of the term, *Fletcherian.* Whether Shakespeare had any hand in its original is not here at issue.

I see no good reason to doubt that Theobald had got hold of the Moseley manuscript, or copies of it, and acted, if not sensibly, at least in good faith. He was capable of making peculiar decisions. On one occasion "a Gentleman, a Watch maker in the City," brought him a play, which was bad until Theobald "created it anew." He considered this just grounds for appropriation and, when the watchmaker protested, he threatened to print the original play, "and leave the World to judge of [its] Grammar, Concord, or English."[20] Even Theobald's account of the provenance of the Cardennio manuscript, savoring though it does of cock-and-bull and tending ot discredit his whole story, may have a reasonable explanation. One of the copies of the play, he said, had survived as the property of Shakespeare's illegitimate daughter. The lady is otherwise unknown, but possibly Mary Davenant is indi-

[20] See Theobald's own self-righteous address to the reader, *The Perfidious Brother,* 1715.

cated. As the widow of Sir William Davenant, active about the theatre long after her husband's death, she is not at all unlikely to have possessed such a relic. In the early eighteenth century Sir William Davenant was rumored to have been Shakespeare's illegitimate son: Theobald may have been guilty only of misconstruing and elaborating common gossip. Of course the best evidence of Theobald's *bona fides* is the fact that records of the early history of the Cardennio play, with its Shakespearean associations, were unknown to him and his contemporaries and were therefore unavailable as grounds upon which to base a fraud. It is also well worth noting that Theobald was willing to exhibit the old manuscript upon which *Double Falsehood* was based.[21]

The episode is pertinent for several reasons. It illustrates the lack of respect accorded original manuscripts even by those who should have known better. It illustrates the fact that even as late as 1727 a "lost" Elizabethan play might be presented to the theatrical and reading public in metamorphosed form. It illustrates, also, to what extent the process of adaptation can conceal the quality of underlying work.[22] Even Theobald's direct admission has been much doubted. Except for the admission, we have in the *Cardennio-Double Falsehood* episode an instance of the very thing I am trying to prove.

THE CASE OF
JOHN FORD–SIR ROBERT HOWARD

Sir Robert Howard's pseudohistorical drama *The Great Favourite, or The Duke of Lerma,* produced and published

[21] A letter in which he makes the offer is printed in *Historical Mss. Comm.,* vol 29, pt. 6, p. 20. I owe this reference to my colleague Mr. John Cadwalader.

[22] There is ample illustration of this in the Restoration adaptations of which the parent plays have survived.

in 1668, has surprised critics with its excellence. D. D. Arundell, its editor, calls the play "daringly successful in its novel untragic seriousness," and praises especially its power of characterization.[23] Allardyce Nicoll remarks that "the pure Maria with the complicated touches in her psychology, and the young king, make up a story that causes us to think more highly of Dryden's collaborator, enemy and friend, than his other works would have warranted."[24] And Montague Summers concurs: ". . . Howard shows a genius, which to my mind informs the whole play, but which save for *The Duke of Lerma* might have been denied him."[25]

Whence, we must ask, came sudden *inspiration* to a playwright whose previous plays had been consistently mediocre? Howard's contemporaries asked the very question, and answered it with a charge that his play had been stolen.[26] In *A Defence of an Essay of Dramatic Poesy* Dryden voices current suspicion with skillful innuendo: ". . . he [Howard] gives me the compellation of 'The Author of a *Dramatic Essay*,' which is a little discourse in dialogue, for the most part borrowed from the observations of others. Therefore, that I may not be wanting to him in civility, I return his compliment by calling him 'The Author of *The Duke of Lerma*.'" In publishing the play, Howard felt obliged to answer the rumors. His answer is thus glossed by Summers: "A play called *The Duke of Lerma,* had been left with the King's

---

[23] D. D. Arundell, *Dryden and Howard, 1664–1668. The Text of . . . The Duke of Lerma* (Cambridge, 1929), p. 208.

[24] A Nicoll, *A History of Restoration Drama,* 2nd ed (Cambridge, 1928), p. 127.

[25] M. Summers, *The Playhouse of Pepys* (New York, 1935), p. 178.

[26] It is odd that modern critics have been so trusting: C. N. Thurber, in his remarks prefacing his edition of *The Committee, Univ. of Ill. Studies in Lang. and Lit.,* 7 (1921), 29, like the rest, confines himself to praise of the exceptional merit of *The Great Favourite.*

Company to dispose of as they pleased. This was submitted to Howard for his opinion, who when he read it found the script frankly impossible although the historical events certainly gave opportunity for a good drama. Thereupon Charles Hart, knowing that Sir Robert was going into the country, persuaded him to employ his leisure on a piece on the same subject.[27]" Compare the amiable interpretation with Howard's own statement:

> For the subject I came accidentally to write upon it. For a gentleman brought a play to the King's Company, called *The Duke of Lerma,* and by them I was desired to peruse it, and return my opinion, whether I thought it fit for the stage. After I had read it, I acquainted them that in my judgment it would not be of much use for such a design, since the contrivance scarce would merit the name of a plot (and some of that assisted by a disguise), and it ended abruptly: and on the person of Philip the 3 there was fixed such a mean character, and on the daughter of the Duke of Lerma such a vicious one, that I could not but judge it unfit to be presented by any that had a respect, not only to princes, but indeed to either man or woman.
>
> And about that time, being to go into the country, I was persuaded by Mr Hart to make it my diversion there, that so great a hint might not be lost, as the Duke of Lerma saving himself in his last extremity by his unexpected disguise, which is as well in the true story as in the old play; and besides that and the names, my altering the most part of the characters, and the whole design, made me uncapable to use much more, though perhaps written with higher style and thoughts than I could attain to.

Several thing are clear. However much he might minimize his debt, after the fashion of the Restoration playwright, Howard's *The Great Favourite, or The Duke of Lerma,* is not an original play but an adaptation. Furthermore—and strange that the fact has aroused no curiosity—the piece he

[27] *The Playhouse of Pepys,* p. 176.

187

reworked was an *old play*. An old play in 1668 would probably mean one written before 1642. Since the historical events interpreted in *The Great Favourite* extend to 1629, we have a fairly narrow range for the date of the original play, and a fairly restricted group from which to select the original author.

Among the Moseley manuscripts was a play called *The Spanish Duke of Lerma,* ascribed to Henry Shirley. It is one of the manuscripts which did *not* descend to· Warburton. Howard revised the old manuscript at the request of Charles Hart, and Charles Hart had been a member of the Red Bull company in 1660[28] at the time Moseley wrote his letter to the Master of the Revels at the solicitation of "the gentlemen actors of the Red Bull."[29] To me it seems reasonably clear where Howard's *old play* came from. *The Spanish Duke of Lerma,* I believe, must have been the play. Henry Shirley, however, could not have been its author.

Henry Shirley is known to us as a dramatist only by the four titles entered in the Stationers' Register in 1653, and by a single extant drama, *The Martyred Soldier,* published in 1638. *The Martyred Soldier* itself may be a work of collaboration;[30] however, we have no choice but to estimate Henry Shirley's powers as a dramatist by this play. *The Martyred Soldier* is a quaint religious drama, rudimentary in characterization and rude in style. Howard would never have admitted that any play by the same hand that produced this one was "perhaps written with higher style and thoughts" than he could attain to.[31]

[28] A. Nicoll, *Restoration Drama,* p. 269.

[29] See above, p. 177.

[30] A. M. Clark, *Thomas Heywood* (Oxford, 1931), pp. 295–300.

[31] The Duke of Lerma died in 1625, Henry Shirley in 1627, but the original author of *The Great Favourite* was aware of the liaison between Philip IV and the actress Maria Calderon (see H. A. Rennert, *The Spanish*

Few playwrights active between 1629 and 1642 would have won such a tribute from Sir Robert Howard, who was an intelligent critic although one predisposed to judge harshly of any but the more refined school of playwriting. James Shirley[32] and Davenant may be eliminated as unlikely to have left available seizable property. Of those who remain, Massinger and Ford are the most likely candidates, and Ford I am sure is our man. If Henry Shirley had anything to do with the original of Howard's play, it must have been as author of a comic underplot which Howard has expunged. More probably, one of Ford's[33] plays had simply been inserted among the relics of Henry Shirley, and had been entered in the Register under the latter's name. This is precisely what happened to Massinger's *Parliament of Love,* entered by Moseley in the Register, 29 June 1660, as by William Rowley,

---

Stage in the Time of Lope de Vega [New York, 1909], p. 164, n. 1). Maria Calderon, as Arundell points out, was the historical original of Maria, daughter of Lerma, in the play. A hint in the last scene indicates that the playwright was aware that Maria Calderon bore Philip a son. John of Austria was born 17 April 1629. This touch might have been added by Howard, but the date of the historical ingredients alone tends to eliminate Henry Shirley as original author.

[32] James Shirley's *The Politician* is entered immediately above *The Spanish Duke of Lerma* in the Stationers' Register, and the identity of surnames would have encouraged clerical error. However, if *The Spanish Duke of Lerma* had been James Shirley's we would probably have its licensing record, and it would probably have been published (as was *The Politician*) in 1655. Shirley was cooperating with Moseley in the issuing of his plays (see *Six New Playes,* 1653).

[33] Three plays by Ford were among the Moseley manuscripts, and the title of one of these, *Beauty in a Trance,* is applicable to Howard's play, if we read *trance* in one of its seventeenth-century meanings as a state of suspended judgment or indecision. However, to suppose this play Howard's original, we must assume that *two* plays had been written on the Lerma story, and must ignore the fact that *Beauty in a Trance* is listed in his collection by Warburton.

apparently because associated with two of Rowley's plays.[34]

The Great Favourite, or The Duke of Lerma bears the stamp of Ford in its plot materials, its characters, and its style. The design of the play is simple. The Duke of Lerma tries to recover his lost power in Spain by prostituting his lovely daughter Maria to young Philip IV. Maria becomes the King's mistress only in report. She sacrifices reputation and filial love and duty in order to save the King from her father's machinations. Philip makes Maria his Queen at last, and Lerma wins immunity from punishment by donning the cardinal's hat which he has secretly obtained from the Pope. Let us observe at once that an elaborate fiction has been grafted upon history in this plot: the historical Duke of Lerma had a son pitted against him, but no daughter. The fiction, even upon first impression, is suggestive of Ford, but we need not depend upon impressions.

In his use of plot materials Ford shows an exceptionally narrow range. He constantly repeats himself. We are justified, then, in drawing tentative conclusions when we discover in Ford's known plays every situation and every major character of *The Great Favourite*. Its plot is a variation of the main plot of Ford's *The Fancies Chaste and Noble,* wherein Castamela plays the part of Maria, her brother Livio the part of Lerma, and the Marquis of Sienna (and his nephew) the part of Philip IV. The resemblance in theme of the two plays is basic, and it is a theme that gave Ford a chance to employ his favorite trick. Ford loves to expose chastity to danger, and to let its loss or preservation hang perilously in the bal-

---

[34] *The Nonesuch,* and *The Book of the Four Honorable Loves.* It is possible that the error may apply in the opposite way and that all three of the plays were Massinger's. W. Rowley's name seems to have been affixed to the copy of *The Parliament of Love* listed by Warburton. Moseley made additional errors, but I believe his ascriptions of authorship are never intentionally fraudulent.

ance while onlookers (both among the characters in the play and the members of the audience) are compelled to believe the worst. Even the details of his methods of plot-making appear. Maria, like Spinella in *The Lady's Trial,* withdraws from actual sight while under a moral cloud, to reappear when it is convenient for her to do so. Unlike most of the situations in the play, Lerma's device of escaping punishment by claiming papal jurisdiction has an historical basis, so that we should not expect its occurrence elsewhere in Ford. But the equivalent of this situation does indeed occur, in act III of *'Tis Pity She's a Whore,*[35] where a cardinal, claiming papal jurisdiction, saves from punishment a contemptible murderer.

Just as striking is the Fordian nature of the characters of *The Great Favourite,* with their bursts of vehemence alternating with sudden moods of tenderness; with their propensity to weep and speak on bended knees, yet curious capacity for intellectual calm. Lerma himself is one of Ford's impudent but admirable sinners. Maria is one of his seductive heroines, responding ambiguously to the love of a man of high station and therefore suspected of unchastity. She most nearly resembles Castamela of *The Fancies,* but we are reminded too of Flavia of the same play, Spinella of *The Lady's Trial,* Bianca of *Love's Sacrifice,* and Penthea of *The Broken Heart.* Philip is the typical prince of Ford's plays, like Palador in *The Lover's Melancholy*—one whom thwarted love has numbed to a lethargy (the word used by Ford and the word used in *The Great Favourite*). Medina is the character so familiar in Ford—railing at a woman for a lustful act which she has committed only in his own evil imaginings. All have that psychological complexity so typical of John Ford, so untypical of Sir Robert Howard.

And finally the style. With the first speech of the play, the

[35] Lerma became a cardinal in 1618. *'Tis Pity* may have preceded *The Spanish Duke of Lerma,* which probably dates between 1630 and 1634.

Prologue, over, we want to write "Exit Howard and enter Ford":

> Repulse upon repulse, like waves thrown back,
> That slide to hang upon obdurate rocks—
> The King shot ruin at me, and there lies
> Forgiving all the world but me alone,
> As if that Heaven too, as well as he,
> Had scratched me out of numbers. At the last
> He turned his feeble eyes away from me,
> As dying men from sins that had misled 'em,
> Blasting my hopes and theirs that hang upon me.
> Thus all those mightly merits of my family
> Are going to his grave, there to be buried.
> And I myself have hung upon his frowns,
> Like dew upon a cloud, till shaken off
> In a cold shower and frozen as it fell,
> Starving my growth with this untimely frost.
> But—I fondly prate away my thoughts,
> Till I have made 'em nothing—like myself.
> See—Here are the parts of my full ruin.
> These decayed outhouses show the chief building
> Wants reparation....

A case for Ford could be argued solely on the basis of verbal parallels—a remarkable fact considering that we have before us a sophisticated text. In discussing the authorship of *The Queen* and *The Spanish Gipsy*,[36] H. Dugdale Sykes has analysed Ford's diction and used words of frequent occurrence as a test of authorship. Such a test must be applied cautiously, but let us observe that many of the words specified by Sykes occur as commonly in *The Great Favourite* as in Ford's acknowledged plays and in those claimed for him on stylistic grounds. In speaking of Ford's partiality for the contractions *t'ee* for *to you* and *d'ee* for *do you,* Sykes affirms "This of it-

---

[36] *Sidelights on Elizabethan Drama* (London, 1924).

self is almost sufficient to prove Ford's presence, for no other dramatist of the time habitually adopts these abbreviations."[37] The contraction *d'ee* for *do you* occurs in *The Great Favourite*. Sykes has noted Ford's fondness for the phrase *traitor to honour, traitor to friendship,* etc. In *The Great Favourite* occur the lines,

> ... dost thou swell that art my creature?
> Thy breath is nurtured from my bounty:
> Why art thou then a traitor to my trust[38]

The words *bounty* and *creature,* incidentally, are in Syke's list of Ford's favorites. Parallels such as these may be explained away as accidental and inconclusive. There is one, however, which cannot be thus dismissed.

Ford habitually speaks of weakness and vice as infections, employing the metaphor in every play, not once but several times. Observe:

> Thou hast brought back a worse infection with thee,—
> Infection of thy mind.   (*The Broken Heart,* III. iv)
> The court, it does infect me with the sloth
> Of sleep and surfeit.   (*The Lover's Melancholy,* II. i)
>   I wish Heaven
> Or my infected honour white again.   (*Perkin Warbeck,* I. iii)
>   ... my infected fate
> Has driven these to seek more healthful airs.
>   (*The Great Favourite,* I. i)
> ... Pride, the dropsy of infected souls
> That swelled 'em first, then burst 'em.
>   (*The Great Favourite,* II. i)

When the vice is lust, the infection induces corruption, usually specified as leprosy. Observe again:

---

[37] Ibid., p. 188, but actually Brome also employs these contractions.

[38] Act III, scene iii. See also "traitor to my prince's soul" (IV. i), "what a traitor is my love" (II. ii).

Beg Heaven to cleanse the leprosy of lust
That rots thy soul.
>   (*'Tis Pity She's a Whore*, I. i)

Get from me strumpet, infamous whore, leprosy of my blood.
>   (*Love's Sacrifice*, III. i)

A whorish itch infects thy blood, a leprosy of raging lust.
>   (*The Fancies*, IV. i)

... set your soul free from that gilded frame
Whose unseen rottenness corrupts it.
>   (*The Great Favourite*, IV. i)

'Tis pity forces me to this violence—
The pity of thy blood, I had a share in,
Before it was infected with this leprosy....
>   (*The Great Favourite*, IV. i)

Revealed to us here is something more than verbal parallelism: it is a habit of mind.

The passage last quoted continues:

The pity of thy youth, thy beauteous youth,[39]
Like a fair flower plucked up by the root
When 'twas but newly budding, before time
Could show it to the world how sweet it was.

Are not these the very cadences of Ford? Or the following:

Feigned accusations and a little time
Will kill all wonder—which is shorter lived
Than dreams of children, or old women's tales.
>   (*The Great Favourite*, IV. ii)

... what wit or art
Could counsel, I have practis'd; but, alas,
I find all these but dreams, and old men's tales.
>   (*'Tis Pity She's a Whore*, I. iii)

That script which Sir Robert found *frankly impossible* did indeed contain a higher style than he could attain to. Some

[39] Compare "This youth, this fair-faced youth ..." in *Lover's Melancholy*, I.i.

passages were transformed into couplets, and some no doubt chastened and clarified in the regrettable manner of Restoration adaptation, but others, I belive, remained virtually untouched, and still sound with the chime of Ford's melancholy music.

What would the original play have been like—before censored by Howard? Maria, says he in his preface, was too *vicious.* Yet speeches by Maria, descended intact, I should guess, from the original play, are quite virtuous.

> He talkt to me of nothing but of goodness,
> And when he spoke of that, (as he must needs)
> He named my mother, and by chance I wept.

In Ford's play Maria, like Bianca in *Love's Sacrifice,* might well have been both vicious and virtuous: Howard had only to delete the vicious side. Lerma's attitude to his daughter, whom he describes as ". . . sweeter than the spring wreath'd in the arms of budding flowers . . . ," may in the original play have been even more sinister than in *The Great Favourite,* and on moral grounds some of Howard's alterations were probably justified. In imagination we can reconstruct that original play which "ended abruptly," though we wish the exercise were unnecessary. As it is, I feel sure that admirers of John Ford have another play to read.

In the next section, I shall canvass the possibility that Mr. Hart passed out manuscripts for revision, not only to Howard, but to John Dryden.

THE CASE OF RICHARD BROME—JOHN DRYDEN

Brome manuscripts should have proved useful to Restoration playwrights. When the latter wrote comedy of humors, they praised Jonson but followed the manner of Brome. Brome's comedies are only superficially akin to Jonson's;

essentially they are, although skillful and entertaining, decidedly guilty plays: always the action spins on an axis of sexual dereliction. Brome is less a Jonson in buckram than a Ford in motley.

It will be necessary to describe a feature of Brome's formula.[40] In *The City Wit,* Josina attempts to employ her own husband (disguised) as pimp and paramour. In *The Northern Lass,* Constance is confused with a prostitute of the same name; when she goes mad with love, she imagines herself with child. In *The Weeding of Covent Garden,* Dorcas poses as a prostitute. In *The Novella,* Victoria poses as a Venetian courtesan and places her virginity on sale at an exorbitant rate. In *The Sparagus Garden,* Annabel pretends to have been seduced, and uses a pillow in order to feign pregnancy. In *A Mad Couple Well Matched,* Lady Thrivewell twice appears in the light of an adulteress. In *The Damoiselle,* Alice is courted in what purports to be a bagnio where virginity is offered as a lottery prize. In *The Court Beggar,* Lady Strangelove's habit of dalliance almost leads to her being ravished, whereupon she falls in love with the would-be ravisher. In earlier comedy, prostitutes were wont to pose as ladies; in Brome's comedy, ladies prose as prostitutes. His heroines all touch pitch. The audience is treated to a display of chastity in jeopardy or under suspicion,[41] and the language of the masquerading ladies is too convincingly coarse. Add a usurious old guardian with designs upon his ward's inheritance; a shopkeeping husband and wife prone to adultery; an assortment of bankrupts, blades, foolish citizens, and eccentrics; and a dialogue that is gruff,[42] animated,

[40] In his best comedies, *The Antipodes* and *The Jovial Crew,* Brome departs from his own formula.

[41] As in Ford; see above, pp. 190–191.

[42] Brome uses more "strengtheners," I believe, than does any other playwright. Innumerable sentences begin with *S'lid* and end with *troe, ha, I*

colloquial, full of tags and of puns and similitudes upon sex—and you have the typical comedy of Richard Brome.

Not every Restoration comedy that follows the Bromean formula am I claiming as a redaction of a Bromean manuscript. The plays to be discussed have survived a careful process of elimination.[43]

In 1675 R. Bentley published *The Mistaken Husband,* with the following note:

> This Play was left in Mr. Dryden's hands many years since: The Author of it was unknown to him, and return'd not to claim it; 'Tis therefore to be presum'd that he is dead.
>
> After twelve years expectation, Mr. Dryden gave it to the Players, having upon perusal of it, found that it deserv'd a better Fate than

warrant you, etc. *Phew, whew,* etc., are common, and such words as *devil, coxcomb, hang, claw,* and *kick,* occur with abnormal frequency.

[43] A play which should not be eliminated from consideration, perhaps, is the old-fashioned, anonymous comedy, *The Factious Citizen, or The Melancholy Visioner,* 1685 (originally published as *Mr. Turbulent,* 1682). It is Bromean in plot materials and characters, and occasionally even in style; but if based on an older text, it has been extensively rewritten. John Wilson's *The Cheats,* 1664, may be an adaptation of a manuscript original. Although the first of Wilson's four plays, it is the most professional among them. To contemporary charges that he had stolen the play, Wilson's reply is curious: "I am in possession, and a bare 'they say', without showing it, will not be sufficient to evict me out of it" ("The Author to the Reader"). M. Nahm's edition, 1934, proves that there are elements in the text dependent upon the writings (1660) and probable sayings of Heydon, a Rosicrucian, but this does not preclude the possibility of an earlier play as the original. (I am inclined to reject *The Hectors,* 1655, named by Dr. Nahm, as the source, since the resemblances seem purely generic.) If there was a manuscript original, I should suspect from the style of *The Cheats* the presence of Middleton rather than of Brome. The fate of Middleton's MS *The Puritan Maid, Modest Wife, and Wanton Widow* challenges attention. Part of the title fits the non-Gallic portion of Betterton's *The Amorous Widow,* ca. 1670 (pub. 1706), but the title in its entirety fits no Restoration play that I have read. The title occurs in Warburton's list, and the MS may have escaped earlier attention.

to be buried in obscurity: I have heard him say, that finding a Scene wanting, he supply'd it; and many have affirm'd, that the stile of it is proper to the Subject, which is what the French call Basse Comedy....[44]

Dryden never directly contradicted Bentley's statement, and the tendency has been to accept it as true. Saintsbury, however, was skeptical. He included the play in his edition—with the following interesting comment: "But the verse does not seem to me to be Dryden's, nor the phrase, nor the cast of thought; in particular, the facture of the blank verse strikes my ear as wholly different from his: indeed I should set it down as decidedly older than his time."[45] Saintsbury asks why anyone should have given Dryden a play in 1663 before he himself was known as a dramatist. He might also have asked what professional dramatist (for *The Mistaken Husband* is assuredly the work of a professional) was giving away plays in 1663.

The text of *The Mistaken Husband* itself supplies the clue to the mystery. Bentley was misleading only in a single detail, and that detail one in which he himself had probably been misled.[46] In act III, scene ii, occurs the following casual allusion:

> ... The Thames is frozen above-Bridge, Sir, and
> Sackcloth-Towns are built upon't: 'tis such a Season, Sir.
> Zeal cannot warm a man: for a Fanaticks Teeth, as he

[44] "The Bookseller to the Reader."

[45] Scott and Saintsbury, *Works of John Dryden,* VIII (Edinburgh, 1882), 647.

[46] He says the play was left in Dryden's hands, and *assumes* it was left by the author, as it has been assumed that the Lerma play (see above, p. 187) was left in Howard's hands *by the author,* but in neither case is the one who delivered the manuscript explicitly identified as the author. In both cases, it is likely that Charles Hart was parceling out Moseley manuscripts.

Pass'd by just now, chattered, as if one had plaid a Tune
On the Gridiron.

The Thames had not been frozen over since the winter of
1634-35[47] (when Dryden was a toddler in Northampton-
shire), and the lines would scarcely have been written into a
play as late as 1663 or 1675 by Dryden or anyone else. There is
an allusion to the great frost of 1634-35 in Brome's *The Sparagus Garden,* act II, scene ii: "Heyday! so last frost she long'd
to ride on one of the Dromedaries over the Thames, when
great men were pleas'd to goe over it a foote." The manuscript "left in Mr. Dryden's hands," the author of which was
"unknown to him," was probably written about the same time
as *The Sparagus Garden,* ca. 1635, and I believe the author
was Richard Brome.

The Mistaken Husband follows the Brome formula: in
both materials and style it resembles his known comedies.
Mrs. Manley, after seven years of unconsummated marriage,
cohabits with an impostor whom she mistakes for her husband.
The cheat discovered, she prefers the impostor to the husband.
A divorce and second marriage[48] permit her to remain in
technical possession of her "virtue." This is precisely Brome.
Dryden's part seems to me to have been mainly simplification
of the plot. The frequent parenthetical constructions, the
abrupt and often purposeless alternation of prose with blank
verse ("decidedly older" than Dryden's), and, above all, the
diction, the turn of phrase, the general atmosphere, all spell
Brome[49]—or so I believe. To others I recommend successive

[47] H. B. Wheatley and P. Cunningham, *London Past and Present* (London, 1891), III, 363. There was no great frost between 1635 and 1683.

[48] An unconsummated marriage and a divorce (or the appearance of
such) occur in Brome's *Northern Lass.*

[49] Brome's source may have been the hypothetical Spanish novel upon
which "Don Martin" in le Sieur de Garouville's *L'Amant oissif,* 1671, was

reading of *The Sparagus Garden, The Mistaken Husband,* and *A Mad Couple Well Matched.*

I pass to what I consider a more interesting possibility—that not one manuscript but two were left with Dryden, and that *The Wild Gallant* is also an adaptation of a lost play by Brome.

Let Dryden himself offer the first testimony in the case: "The Plot was not Originally my own: but so Alter'd by me (whether for the better or worse, I know not) that, whoever the Author was, he could not have challeng'd a Scene of it."[50] In his excellent discussion of Dryden's sources N. B. Allen glosses the playwright's words as follows: "Dryden does not necessarily mean by this that he had any one source for the whole play. If he does refer to any one previous work, it is probably to the *Decameron,* to Shirley's *Lady of Pleasure,* or to Brome's *Sparagus Garden,* from each of which, it will be shown, he got a definite suggestion."[51] I must disagree. Of none of the three works mentioned need Dryden have said "whoever the Author was." Clearly, I believe, *one* work is referred to—*a play which Dryden has "alter'd."* Mention in the Prologue of "a Spanish plot"—actually an allusion[52] to

---

based. M. Summers has noted the resemblance between the story of "Don Martin" and that of *The Mistaken Husband,* and remarks the difficulty of considering "Don Martin," 1671, as the source of a play of 1663 (M. Summers, *Dryden. The Dramatic Works,* 6 vols. [London, 1931–1932], IV, 5). M. Summers (ibid., IV, 463) points out that *The Mistaken Husband* was evidently written for an open platform stage, as likewise was *The Wild Gallant.* An open platform stage was still available in 1663 but not in 1675.

[50] "Preface," *The Wild Gallant,* 1667.

[51] Ned B. Allen, *The Sources of John Dryden's Comedies* (Ann Arbor, 1935), p. 9 n.

[52] The fact admits of no doubt. The point was made by Allison Gaw, "Tuke's 'Adventures of Five Hours' in Relation to the 'Spanish plot' and to John Dryden," *Publ. Univ. Pennsylvania, Series in Philology and Literature,*

Tuke's *Adventures of Five Hours* adapted from Coello—has led nearly all commentators on *The Wild Gallant* to assume a source in Spanish drama, despite the explicit statement in the same Prologue, "This play is English, and the Growth your own."[53] Dryden has as good as told us that he has adapted an English play whose author was unknown to him. Had the original play been in print, it would long since have been identified; *ergo* it reached Dryden in manuscript. The case of *The Wild Gallant* offers an exact parallel with that of *The Mistaken Husband*—except that this time Dryden himself, not Bentley, is our informant.

The Wild Gallant, like *The Mistaken Husband,* follows the Brome formula. Lady Constance is the heroine who touches pitch. In the true Bromean manner, she simulates pregnancy with a pillow in order to win through to marriage with her gallant. The scene in which the male members of the Nonsuch family are made to believe they are pregnant has frequently bemused admirers of Dryden, but the scene would surprise no one in a comedy by Brome. Too Bromean to be mere imitations are Shopkeeper Bibber and his wife Frances—to whom gallants are indebted "for Chamber-rent, and Diet, and many a good thing besides, that shall be nameless":

Lov.   Nay but good Landlady—
Franc. Will good Landlady set on the Pot, as they say; or make the Jack goe; then I'll hear you.
Bib.   Now she's too much on t'other hand: hold your prating Frances. . . .
Franc. I did but lay the Law open to him, as they say, whereby to get our money in: but if you knew how he has us'd me, Husband.

---

14 (1917), 1–61. N. B. Allen, *Sources of Dryden's Comedies,* pp. 2–7, has reminded scholars of Gaw's findings.

[53] "Prologue to *The Wild Gallant,* as it was first Acted."

Bib.   Has he us'd you Frances; put so much more into his Bill
           for Lodging.[54]

The Wild Gallant, indifferently successful in 1663, was revived with alterations in 1667, and the text we have is that
of the revival. Since even in the version of 1663 the source play
had been "so alter'd . . . that, whoever the Author was, he
could not have Challeng'd a Scene of it," we might expect,
in the version of 1667, little of Brome's language to remain
(assuming for the moment that Brome is our man). Certainly
The Wild Gallant has been rewritten more completely than
The Mistaken Husband, and many of the smarter portions[55]
are wholly in Dryden's language; nevertheless, I believe that
the hand of Brome is frequently traceable. I shall limit myself
to a single illustration. Speeches which frequently repeat the
term of address seemed to Brome so irresistibly funny that
he employed the device at least once in nearly every comedy.

Thomas your hopes are vaine, *Thomas* in seating mee here to
overreach, or underreach any body. I am weary of this Mechanick
course *Thomas;* and of this courser habit, as I have told you
divers and sundry times *Thomas,* and indeed of you *Thomas*
that confine me to 't . . .   *A Mad Couple Well Matched,* ii. i.
     I am a poore Tradesman Mr. *Crasie,* keep both a Linnen and a
Wollen Drapers shop, Mr. *Crasie,* according to my name, Mr.
Crasie, and would be loth to lend my money, Mr. *Crasie,* to be

---

[54] Act 1, scene i. Compare Bumpsey and Magdalen in *The Damoiselle,*
Saleware and Alicia in *A Mad Couple Well Matched,* Brittleware and
Rebecca in *The Sparagus Garden,* etc.

[55] The contrasting styles in *The Wild Gallant* have compelled Allen
(*Sources of Dryden's Comedies,* p. 22) to infer that the "Jonsonian" portions
of the play may have been drafted by Dryden before 1658—an unnecessary
inference if there was a manuscript original. Similar disparity in its parts
occurs in Etherege's *Love in a Tub,* but here the more primitive portions
do indeed seem to date from the Interregnum period.

laught at among my neighbours, Mr. *Crasie,* as you are Mr. *Crasie.*
The City Wit, I. ii.

No indeed *John Brittleware;* the Asparagus has done its part; but you have not done your part *John;* and if you were an honest man, *John,* you would make sir *Hughes* words good of the Asparagus, and be kinder to me: you are not kind to your own wife *John ...* *The Sparagus Garden,* III. viii.

O my deare *Bump!* Art thou there? Thou mayst kisse, and forgive me all over too, for any harm, or dishonesty, though the place be as they say—at a word, *Bump.* Thou mayst believe me, I came but to learn carriage of the Body, not to carry no bodies body, but my owne body, *Bump.* No truely, truely *Bump.* . . . .
The Damoiselle, v. i.

My Mistriss commends her best love unto your Worship, and desires to know how your Worship came home last Night, and how your Worship have rested, and how your Worship does this morning? She hopes the best of your Worships health, and would be glad to see your Worship at your Worships best leasure.
The Northern Lass, I. vi.

Yes ant like your Lordship upon some private notice given to me an't like your Lordship, that she was at a private lodging ant like your Lordship, with a private friend ant like your Lordship, over I went, and found her abed ant like your Lordship, and Mr. *Bellamy* even ready to go to bed to her ant like your Lordship.
A Mad Couple Well Matched, v. i.

And't please your worship, it was seventeen pounds and a Noble, yesterday at noon, your worship knows: And then your worship came home ill last night, and complain'd of your worships head; and I sent for 3 Dishes of Tea for your good worship, and that was six pence more, and please your worship's honor.
The Wild Gallant, I. i.

My Cinque I play here Sir, my Cater here, Sir: now for you, Sir, but first I'll drink to you Sir; upon my faith I'll do you reason, Sir: mine was thus full Sir: pray mind your play, Sir . . .
The Wild Gallant, I. i.

Here *William*! this is a Judgement, as they say, upon you *William*; for trusting Wits, and calling Gentlemen to the Tavern *William*. *The Wild Gallant*, v. i.[56]

To me the style of large portions of *The Wild Gallant* seems to resemble Brome's more than Dryden's in his later comedies. Dryden himself placed small value upon his early work. He must have believed that he had done enough original writing in *The Wild Gallant* to establish ownership, but he disparaged the play; and he never even claimed *The Mistaken Husband*. There is nothing intrinsically improbable, or discreditable, about Dryden's beginning his playwriting career by cobbling the work of predecessors.[57]

[56] To play the game through, I quote the following from *The Mistaken Husband*, I. ii:

Hazzard. Honest Thomas, how dost thou? how hast done this long time honest Thomas?

Thomas. Troth Sir, as you see, I want Clothes, and money, and the best can do no more Sir . . . And truly Sir, I cannot know you by instinct: it may be you know me, but truly Sir I never saw you before.

Hazzard. Thomas, I did not think you would so easily forget your friends; not know me Thomas!

[57] I have not tried to relate the two plays discussed with specific titles by Brome. In both cases the original author's name seems to have been unknown to Dryden, so that the manuscripts could not have contained the author's name, as those attributed to Brome by Moseley must have done. Considerable work by Brome must have remained unprinted. He was once under contract to supply three plays a year to the Salisbury Court Theatre. Such plays as *The Woman's Masterpiece*, or even *Marriage without a Man* (given as a second title to "Shakespeare's" *Iphis and Ianthe*) may have been his: I mention these titles for illustration because they would fit the originals of the Dryden plays. Brome manuscript may underlie a few of the comedies of Shadwell, Behn, and D'Urfey. Most of the material must be highly speculative, but I believe that D'Urfey's *Richmond Heiress, or a Woman Once in the Right* levied upon Brome's lost *Wit in Madness*. The fate of the Massinger plays, some of which may have been rewritten as heroic tragedies, also challenges investigation.

THE CASE OF "SHAKESPEARE AND DAVENPORT" –BANCROFT AND MOUNTFORT

All problems concerning Shakespeare are, of course, momentous, and involved. The least momentous are not always the least involved, and the reader of what ensues may have to call upon certain reserves of patience.

Among the titles entered in the Stationers' Register by Humphrey Moseley on 9 September 1653 appears

Henry the first, & Hen: the 2nd, by Shakespeare & Davenport,[58]

and among those entered on 29 June 1660

The History of King Stephen
Duke Humphrey, a Tragedy ⎱ by Will: Shakspeare
Iphis & Ianthe or a Marriage without a Man ⎰
The Fatal Brothers, a Tragedy ⎱ by Robt Davenport[59]
The Politick Queen, or murther will out ⎰

Since the long reign of King Stephen intervened between those of the two Henry's, *Henry the First and Henry the Second* seems an extremely unlikely title for a play; and as Moseley in 1653 was saving fees by entering two plays as one, it is fairly obvious that he was doing so in the present instance. The inference is supported by the occurrence in Warburton's list of the title, "Henry ye 1st by Will Shakespear & Rob. Davenport."[60] Before Warburton's time the *Henry the Second* manuscript had evidently become separated from its fellow.

As one speculates about the titles listed above, one's first

---

[58] G. E. B. Eyre, *A Transcript of the Registers of the Worshipful Company of Stationers,* 3 vols. (London, 1913–1914), I, 429.

[59] Ibid., II, 271.

[60] Brit. Mus. MS Lansdowne 807. See W. W. Greg, "The Bakings of Betsy," p. 230.

thought is that *Duke Humphrey* may have been a play in which the best parts of *Henry VI, Parts I and II,* had been salvaged,[61] and that *Henry the First, King Stephen, and Henry the Second* may have formed a lost Shakespearean trilogy. The latter theory, however, must be quickly abandoned. It is unlikely that an entire historical trilogy should have been written by Shakespeare and escaped all contemporary mention—by Meres, the editors of the first folio, and so forth. Furthermore, *Henry the First* has an earlier record which tends to eliminate Shakespeare as co-author. On 10 April 1624 was licensed for acting by the King's Men "The Historye of Henry the First, written by Damport."[62] This must have been one of the two plays of the 1653 entry. It is true that in 1624 Davenport may have been reworking an older play, but such a play is more likely to have belonged to their rivals than to Shakespeare's company. Pursuing the trail back, we find that in March 1598 Henslowe paid Drayton, Dekker, and Chettle, on behalf of the Admiral's Men, for "the famos wares of henry the fyrste & the prynce of walles," and that even earlier, on 26 May 1597, the Admiral's Men had added to their repertory "harey the firste life & deth."[63] It was an old Admiral's play, *The Death of Robert Earl of Huntington,* 1598, by Chettle and Munday, that Davenport used so freely in writing his *King John and Matilda* at about the same time as *Henry the First* was licensed.

Shakespeare's name could have become attached to the manuscript of *Henry the First* merely because it was evident that it was an adaptation of a play dating from Shakespeare's time. Ultimately, as we have seen, the copy of *Henry the First* aided in the baking of those numerous pies which, we trust,

---

[61] But see below, note 76.

[62] *Dramatic Records of Sir Henry Herbert,* ed. J. Q. Adams (New Haven, 1917), pp. 27–28.

[63] *Henslowe's Diary,* ed. Greg, I, 85, 52.

shortened the life of the Somerset herald. But what of *Henry the Second,* the companion play, which did not descend to Warburton? The connection of Shakespeare's name with this play would be purely adventitious. Not so Davenport's. Where identification is possible, we find that when Moseley smuggled into the Register a second play, it was usually by the same author as the first.[64] *Henry the Second* and another of the Moseley plays by Davenport, *The Politic Queen, or Murder Will Out,* may not be totally lost. In 1693 and 1691, respectively, were published, under peculiar auspices, *Henry the Second, King of England; With The Death of Rosamond. A Tragedy. Acted at the Theatre Royal, By Their Majesties Servants* (which I believe to be a stage version of "Shakespeare and Davenport's" *Henry the Second*), and *King Edward the Third, With The Fall of Mortimer Earl of March. An Historicall Play, As it is Acted at the Theatre-Royal By their Majesties Servants* (which I believe to be a stage version of Davenport's *The Politic Queen*). No name is attached to the publications except that of the actor, William Mountfort, who signed the dedications. The plays were included in the 1720 edition of Mountfort's works, because the editor believed the actor must have had a share in them, "otherwise it cannot be supposed he would have taken the Liberty of Writing Dedications to them"—a moderate view of the liberties taken in Mountfort's day! In fairness to the actor we must add that he never claimed authorship, and may have had a hand in fitting the plays to the Restoration stage.

After the creation of the United Company, a surprising number of fellow actors blossomed forth as authors, or at least sponsors, of play books: Thomas Jevon with *The Devil of a Wife,* 1686; James Carlisle with *The Fortune Hunters,* 1689; Joseph Harris with *The Mistakes,* 1691; Cave Underhill

[64] The survival of Herbert's licensing records enables us to determine the nature of the double entries in the case of most of the Massinger plays.

with *Win Her and Take Her,* 1691; Joe Haynes with *A Fatal Mistake,* 1692. There were others, the most productive of whom were George Powell and William Mountfort. The phenomenon, I believe, has never been discussed in histories of the Restoration stage, but it almost appears that a new variety of "benefit" had been devised, wherein a particular actor was to have "author's rights" to the performance and publication of a particular play, regardless of how he had established possession. Some of the plays are recognizable adaptations; some, at least by Powell and Mountfort, palpably original; while others are of mysterious origin—"presents" by self-abnegating authors who were "contented with applause."[65] A jocularity of tone regarding authorship prevails in the prologues and epilogues, suggesting to me that the actors had found a deposit of plays and were working the vein. The group could boast, if not a first-class playwright, at least a first-class writer of dedications. A uniform fluency marks these, all of which are addressed to men who could acknowledge the honor substantially.

Henry the Second and *Edward the Third* were products of the "movement" sketched above. In the case of the former Mountfort simply signed the dedication, neither claiming nor disclaiming authorship, but in the case of the latter he speaks of the play as a present, and says in his epilogue that

> ...the Author who did this Prepare
> Only expects your Liking for his share.

He may have been referring to an adapter other than himself; otherwise I believe he was being consciously misleading in implying that the author was still alive.

[65] Epilogue to *Win Her and Take Her,* 1691. In the prologue Cave Underhill, signer of the dedication, says, "You have been kinde to most of our young Actors" and "The Profits of this Play to me are given."

Certain errors about the two plays have been dignified by repetition and must be disposed of first. Halliwell-Phillipps in his *Dictionary* said of *Edward the Third* that "the plot is from the English history, with comic underplot, and from a novel called 'The Countess of Salisbury'." If this were true, an early date for the play would be precluded. *The Countess of Salisbury; or The Most Noble Order of the Garter. An Historical Novel. In Two Parts. Done out of French by Mr Ferrand Spence* was not published until 1683. But the statement is in total error. *The Countess of Salisbury* has nothing whatever to do with the *Edward the Third* of 1691. The play is concerned with Queen Isabella and Mortimer. Halliwell-Phillips or his authorities must have supposed that it was upon the same theme as the anonymous *Reign of King Edward the Third,* 1596, in which case *The Countess of Salisbury* would have been a good guess as to its immediate source. Actually, the materials of the play were old enough to be available to Robert Davenport. So also were those of *Henry the Second.* In the case of the latter, one of the sources would have been more likely to be used by Davenport than by any contemporary of Mountfort: "The Deathe of Faire Rosamond," which first appeared in the 1607 edition of *Strange Histories.* In the ballad Rosamond pleads with King Henry to be taken to the wars:

> Nay rather let me, like a Page
>   your shield and Target beare,
> That on my brest the blow may light,
>   that should annoy you there.
> O let me in your Royal Tent
>   prepare your bed at night. . . .[66]

In the play this becomes,

[66] *The Works of Thomas Deloney,* ed. F. O. Mann (Oxford, 1912), p. 299.

> I'll like a Page attend you where you go,
> Run by your side, and Watch you Sleeping hours,
> And in the Fight I'll always meet your Danger:
> I'll step before you as your Fate approaches.[67]

Henry's refusal in the ballad,

> Fair Ladies brooke not bloudy warrs,
> sweet peace their pleasure breede:

is paralleled by Henry's refusal in the play,

> Thy tender Body cannot brook such usage,
> As the Necessity of War throws on us.

A stubborn error to deal with is the attribution of *Henry the Second* and *Edward the Third* to the Restoration physician John Bancroft. All works which go beyond Mountfort as author name Bancroft, usually with surprising confidence. The attribution begins with Charles Gildon,[68] not the most reliable of authorities, and one who was writing after the death of both Mountfort and Bancroft. We can surmise why Gildon hit upon this particular person. When Mountfort was set upon by Lord Mohun and Captain Hill in 1692, Bancroft was called in to attend him, and the physician's testimony figured so largely in the subsequent murder trial that his name was linked thereafter with the actor's. *Henry the Second* was too good a play to have been written by Mountfort,

---

[67] *Henry the Second,* act IV.

[68] *The Lives and Characters of the English Dramatick Poets* (1699), p. 5. Gildon gives Bancroft only *Henry the Second.* In a note upon Gildon, Thomas Coxeter adds *King Edward the Third.* Coxeter would have been justified because as early as October 1692 *The Gentleman's Journal* calls *Henry the Second* a "new Play, by the Author of that call'd Edward the Third" (cf. A. S. Borgman, *The Life and Death of William Mountfort* [Cambridge, Mass., 1935], p. 86n.), and the two plays are evidently from the same hand. Gildon's giving one of the plays to Bancroft and listing the other as anonymous tends to impeach his knowledge of the authorship of either.

and Bancroft himself had written an excellent tragedy. This, I believe, would have sufficed Gildon. Whether such is the explanation of the error is, after all, immaterial: an error has certainly been made.

The Tragedy of Sertorius was publicly acknowledged by Bancroft in 1679; there is no reason why he should have turned to surreptitous authorship years later. Both in type and style *Sertorious* is poles apart from *Henry the Second* and *Edward the Third*. Its scene division is upon rigid classical principles, and its blank verse severely regular: Bancroft is so meticulous with his decasyllables that he seems sometimes to count them on his fingers. The two historical plays attributed to him have an Elizabethan fluidity of structure, and their blank verse is marked by constant use of half-lines and redundant syllables; occasionally it is, like Davenport's, little more than rhythmic prose. It is not, incidentally, the blank verse of Mountfort. In such an obviously original play as Mountfort's *The Injur'd Lovers,* 1688, the verse is irregular enough, but with the irregularity of sheer ineptitude, as witness

> ... the Swain whom
> She affects is streight made hers;
> So they proceed to others in their turn
> Continuing Celebrating for three daies.[69]

If one were to read Davenport's *King John and Matilda,* Bancroft's *Sertorius,* and Mountfort's *Injur'd Lovers,* then turn to *Henry the Second* and *Edward the Third* without previous knowledge of the date of the two plays, one would instantly select Davenport as author in preference to the other two. One would be amazed to learn that *Sertorius* and *The Injur'd Lovers* were coeval in publication with them, *King John and Matilda* earlier by more than sixty years. That

[69] Act II, scene i.

the two plays were something of an apparition in the nineties is conceded in their prologues,[70] and the modern critic is impelled to affirm, "These two plays are both very Elizabethan in character."[71] I shall quote from *King John and Matilda* and from *Henry the Second* passages where similarity in the situations gives the best opportunity for comparison: King John importunes Matilda—

K. Fair *Matilda,*
Mistresse of youth and beauty, sweet as a spring,
And comely as the holy shining Priest
Deckt in his glorious sacerdotall vestment;
Yet heare the passions of a love sick Prince,
And crown thy too too cruel heart with pitty.
   Mat. Yet let fall your too too passionate pleadings,
And crown your royall heart with excellent reason.
   K. Hear me.
   Mat. The Queen will heare you.
   K. Speak but a word that—
   Mat. What?
   K. That may sound like something
That may but busie my strong labouring heart
With hope that thou wilt grant, and every morning
I will walk forth and watch the early Lark,
And at her sweetest note I will protest,
Matilda spake a word was like that note.
   Mat. Oh how you tempt: remember, pray, your vows
To my betroth'd Earl *Robert Huntington;*
Did you not wish, just as the poyson toucht
His manly heart, if ever you again
Laid battery to the fair fort of my unvanquish'd
Vertue, your death might be like his untimely,

---

[70] That of *Henry the Second* appeals to a citizen audience for protection and that of *Edward the Third* asks "Why mayn't the Antient way of Writing please."
[71] A. Nicoll, *Restoration Drama,* p. 158.

And be poyson'd? Oh take heed, sir,
Saints stand upon heavens silver battlements
When Kings make vows, and lay their listening ears
To Princes Protestation.
   K. So did
Matilda swear to live and die a maid,
At which fair Nature like a snail shrunk back,
As loath to hear from one so fair, so foul
A wound: my vow was vain, made without
Recollection of my reason; and yours, Oh madnesse!
For *Huntington,* he like a heap
Of summers dust into his Grave is swept;
And bad vows still are better broke then kept.
   Mat. Alas, great sir! your Queen you cannot make me!
What is it then instructs your tongue? Oh sir!
Lust is but loves well languag'd hypocrite.[72]

King Henry importunes Rosamond—

   King. Why dost thou shun my Love, thou Charming Maid?
Why turn away they Eyes, now they've undone me?
Thou shouldst have hid their killing Fires before:
Too well thy conscious Soul their Lustre knew,
Foresaw the Adoration they'd beget;
Thou shouldst have ever kept 'em from Mankind,
Or mingl'd Pity with their barb'rous Pow'r.
   Rosam. Why will you thus perplex your self and me?
How often have I begg'd you to desist!
Methinks the many times I have deny'd
Might satisfie you your Attempts are vain.
   King. Judge rightly of the Patience of my Love,
With what a meek untir'd Zeal 't has waited,
Born all the cold Rebukes of rigid Virtue,
The harsh Denials of a vigorous Honour,
Still creeping up to what I knew would crush me:
Like the weak Reed against the blust'ring North,

[72] *King John and Matilda,* ed. Bullen, act i, scene i.

That nods and crouches to each angry Blast,
Sinks down o'er-press'd by the insulting Storm;
Yet still it swells, and slowly strives to rise,
To be blown down again.
   Rosam. Oh! why do you pursue me?
   King. Because my Peace has took her flight that way,
And I must follow through this rugged Road
To find it out, though every step I tread
Brings my strict search but nearer to Destruction.
   Rosam. No, King, in vain you lay a Siege;
The Fort's impregnable.
   King. You think my Power's the less because I sue,
Begging that Blessing which I might command.
How easie might I seize the long'd-for Joy;
But Force dissolves the sweetness of the Charm.
Let then my Sufferings urge at last some Hope,
Let cruel Virtue yield but to a Parley,
Grant my Request, and make thy own Conditions.
   Rosam. What can you hope from such a wretched Conquest,
Where all the Spoil is Infamy and Shame?
Why would you soil the Glories of your Life,
In mingling with the Creature you have made?[73]

Davenport was given to word-echoing. Observe in *The City-Night-Cap:*

   1 *Slave.* 'Tis true, though.
   Lor. True, villain! are both now seen in the base act?
   1 *Slave.* Yes, both.
   Lor. Which both?
   1 *Slave.* You and I, sir.
   Omn. How?
   1 *Slave.* Both you and I are seen in the base act,
Slandering spotless honour; an act so base
The barbarous Moor would blush at.
   Phil. D'ye hear him now?

[73] *Henry the Second,* 1693, act II, scene ii.

214

Lor. Out, Slave, wilt thou give ground too? fear works upon 'em.
Did you not both here swear i'th Senate-chamber
You saw them both dishonest?
   1 *Slave.* Then we swore true, sir,
   Lor. I told you 'twas but fear.
   Vero. Swore ye true then, sir, when ye swore
Ye both saw them dishonest?
   1 *Slave.* Yes, marry, did we sir:
For we were both two villians when we saw them,
So we saw them dishonest.[74]

and in *Henry the Second:*

So we must part; there is no Remedy.
   King. 'Tis a sad Truth indeed: Part! 'tis resolv'd!
Alas, I only came to take my leave,
But fain I would have parted Friends with thee,
Because I thought I had no Friend beside.

   Rosa. And could you think parting would make us Friends?
   King. No, but I thought our meeting might.
   Rosa. Then why d'ye talk of parting?
   King. I know not what I talk of; any thing, let us but talk.
   Rosa. Better be silent, sure, than talk of that.
   King. Why must we not then part?
   Rosa. Oh never, *Henry!* I can hold no longer!
Be false, or faithful, I must love thee ever.
If we must part, be't all upon thy Head!
For thus I am resolv'd to live or dye.[75]

At this point the reader may say that, granted the presence of an adapter, the play of 1693 may have been written originally by Davenport, but it may also have been written by some other early dramatist. I must insert the reminder that a manuscript by Davenport called *Henry the Second* disappeared during the Restoration, and that the title of a second

[74] *The City-Night-Cap,* ed. Bullen, act III, scene ii.
[75] Act IV.

such manuscript by Davenport, *The Politic Queen, or Murder Will Out,* exactly fits our second play, *Edward the Third.*

I shall conclude with what must be conceded at least as an interesting coincidence. In 1619 Michael Drayton published his *Poems,* including in the volume *Englands Heroicall Epistles,* the sad avowals of a series of noble and royal lovers. The first in the series are the epistles of Rosamond and King Henry the Second, the second those of King John and Matilda, the third those of Queen Isabella and Mortimer. Here, then, are brought together the themes of *Henry the Second,* 1693, Davenport's *King John and Matilda,* and *Edward the Third,* 1691.[76] Does it not seem likely that Davenport, acting upon the suggestion of the volume of 1619, embarked upon the creation of a series of neo-chronicles—centering upon the loves of the English kings rather than upon their martial exploits, and more in keeping therefore with the softer texture of the Fletcherian era? The *Heroicall Epistles* are not narratives and cannot be considered as "sources" of our three plays, but there is other evidence that Davenport was a reader of Drayton. Drayton's *The Legend of Matilda,* also included in the collection of 1619, contains the following stanza:

> When all that Race in memorie are set,
> And by their Statues, their Atchievements done,
> Which wonne abroad, and which at home did get,
> From Sonne to Sire, from Sire againe to Sonne,
> Grac'd with the spoyles, that gloriously they wonne:
> O, that of Him, it only should be said,
> This was King John, the Murth'rer of a Maid![77]

[76] Possibly Moseley attributed other Davenport plays to Shakespeare. "Duke Humphrey" may treat the story of Humphrey and Elinor Cobham, which also figures in *Englands Heroicall Epistles.*

[77] *The Works of Michael Drayton,* ed. J. W. Hebel, 5 vols. (Oxford, 1931), II, 427.

and Davenport's *King John and Matilda* the following passage:

> There was the last call; to the King commend me,
> And tell him, when in stories he shall stand,
> When men shall read the Conquerors great name,
> Voluptuous *Rufus,* that unkind brother *Beauclark,*
> Comely King *Steven, Henry* the Wedlock-breaker,
> And Lyon-hearted *Richard;* when they come
> Unto his name, with sighs it shall be said,
> *This was King* John—*the murderer of a Maid.*[78]

A satisfactory parallel surely! Note, too, how in mentioning Henry II Davenport reveals what aspect of this king's career most engages his attention. Davenport is thinking not of Henry the reformer, the opponent of Becket, the conqueror of Ireland, but of *Henry the Wedlock-breaker*—the lover of the Fair Rosamond.

CONCLUSION

I trust that I have not merely evoked what Hume considered the quintessence of scepticism—the opinion that the argument can be neither refuted nor believed. I am fully aware of the speculative nature of my discussion and the inconclusiveness of its parts. I personally believe that Sir Robert Howard's *The Great Favourite* is based upon Ford's (not Henry Shirley's) *The Spanish Duke of Lerma,* that Dryden's *The Wild Gallant* and *The Mistaken Husband* are based upon manuscripts by Brome, that *Henry the Second* and *Edward the Third* are based upon Davenport's (not Shakespeare's) *Henry the Second* and Davenport's *The Politic Queen.* I do not expect others to share fully in my belief. On the other hand, I have a reasonable hope that all will not be

[78] Act v, scene ii.

dismissed as a product of coincidence and ingenuity, but that my thesis in general will stand.

I have found that, as the hunter for lost Elizabethan plays works through Restoration territory, game seems to spring up on every hand. I am sure that I have left behind better than I have taken. In the present discussion I have confined my illustrations to Restoration plays about the authorship of which there hovered a demonstrable doubt. I have not quite ranged rampant. Individual discoveries, in any case, will never be very important. A play is made no better by our knowledge that it had an Elizabethan basis, although in a few cases the knowledge might quicken us to the fact that the merit is already there. Usually, we shall find only a somewhat spoiled version of a play by a second-rate Elizabethan: we shall discover only the play which Shakespeare did not write.

My theory, even so, may have a certain utility. Future editors may find it helpful in resolving problems in Restoration texts—puzzling little problems like allusions to the Thames being frozen over when nothing of the kind had occurred for forty years. Future critics may justify their statements that a play is "very Elizabethan in character." There is always the possibility that the new play has been *written over* an old one, and the erasure of the old play is not complete. The later seventeenth-century drama should be viewed against a wider horizon and with an increased alertness. We need as much light as we can get. Restoration drama cannot be understood without a knowledge of Elizabethan drama; in a measure, the converse may also be true.

INDEX

INDEX

INDEX

INDEX

INDEX

INDEX

225

INDEX

INDEX

INDEX

228

Hum
PR
2899
H374

IT